THEY CAL

"PURPLE HEART VALLEY"

A Combat Chronicle of the War in Italy

TEXT AND PHOTOGRAPHS BY
MARGARET BOURKE-WHITE

SIMON AND SCHUSTER · NEW YORK · 1944

ABOUT THE APPEARANCE OF BOOKS IN WARTIME

A recent ruling by the War Production Board has curtailed the use of paper by book publishers in 1944.

In line with this ruling and in order to conserve materials and manpower, we are co-operating by:

1. Using lighter-weight paper, which reduces the bulk of our books substantially.

2. Printing books with smaller margins and with more words to each page. Result fewer pages per book.

Slimmer and smaller books will save paper and plate metal and labor. We are sure that readers will understand the publishers' desire to co-operate as fully as possible with the objectives of the War Production Board and our government.

HALFTONE PLATES MADE BY EAGLE PHOTO-ENGRAVING CO.
MANUFACTURED IN THE UNITED STATES OF AMERICA
BY AMERICAN BOOK–STRATFORD PRESS, INC., N. Y.

For Jessie D. Munger
who in her own quiet way brought
much cheer to the winners of
Purple Hearts in the last world war.

I WISH TO EXPRESS my sincere gratitude to General Brehon Somervell and his associates in the Army Service Forces, who gave me great co-operation in both North Africa and Italy; to Edward Stanley for his patient and invaluable help with the captions; to those unsung heroes in *Life*'s darkroom for their technical assistance; and most of all to the editors of *Life*, first for sending me on this assignment and secondly for their generosity in allowing me to use the photographs in this book.

MARGARET BOURKE-WHITE

Contents

Illustrations

THEY CALLED IT
PURPLE HEART
VALLEY

CHAPTER 1

Over the Lines

"THIS STRIP is really a nerve jerker," Lieutenant Mike Strok called to me over his shoulder.

We were circling above the tiniest airfield I had ever seen. The landing strip was so pocked with shell craters that I did not see how my Grasshopper pilot was going to slip in among them. It was nothing more than the beaten edge of a plowed field, but for the Air OP's, the "Eyes of the Artillery" as they are called in heavy-gun circles, this strip was their most forward operating base.

Lieutenant Strok had to divide his attention between the shell pits below and the sky above. This was because we were landing in the region airmen called Messerschmitt Alley. If an unarmed, unarmored observation plane such as our Cub is attacked, the pilot's means of escape is to outmaneuver the enemy.

"Good idea to make sure there's no Jerry fighter hanging about," said Lieutenant Strok. "If you can see him first, then he doesn't get the chance to blast the daylights out of you."

A final inspection confirmed that the sky was clear, and he brought our tiny Cub to a standstill on a piece of earth as big as a back yard in Brooklyn.

The commanding officer of the field and his ground crew of one ran up to greet us.

The ground crew spoke first. "If that ain't an American girl, then I'm seeing things!" he exclaimed.

The young officer laughed. "Sorry we're out of red carpet," he said. "We live like gypsies up here."

The CO of the Grasshoppers was twenty-six-year-old Captain Jack Marinelli of Ottumwa, Iowa. He was chief pilot and supervisor for a group of artillery liaison pilots who hedgehopped along the front lines in their Cubs, acting as flying observation posts to spot enemy targets

3

and adjust fire for Fifth Army artillery. I had seldom seen a flier who bore less resemblance to Hollywood's idea of a pilot than Captain Marinelli. He looked more like the tractor and hay-machine demonstrator which I learned he had been back in Iowa before the war. He was plump, pleasant, and easygoing. This last characteristic, I was to find, faded as soon as the enemy was in sight. He had the reputation of being the coolest and most resourceful artillery pilot on the Fifth Army front.

Mike Strok explained that I wanted to take airplane pictures of the front, and Captain Marinelli said, "Well, I've just had a call to go out on a mission. There's a *Nebelwerfer* holding up an infantry division and they asked me to go out and try to spot it. She can come along if she wants to."

"Jees, you don't want to take a girl on a mission," said the ground crew of one.

"She'll go if you'll take her," stated Lieutenant Strok.

"What's a *Nebelwerfer?*" I inquired.

"You've heard of a screaming meemie, haven't you? Wicked weapon! It's a multiple mortar: eight-barreled rocket gun."

By the time the screaming meemie was explained to me, I had been strapped into the observer's seat, and the ground crew was adjusting a parachute to my back and shoulders.

Knowing that one of the functions of observer is to watch all quadrants of the sky for enemy planes, I said to the Captain, "I'm not going to make a very good observer for you. Most of the time I'll have my face buried in my camera, and even when I haven't, I'm not sure I'll know the difference between an enemy fighter and one of ours."

"Don't worry about that," Captain Marinelli said. "If you see anything that looks like an airplane, you tell me and I'll decide whether it's a bandit or an angel."

I placed my airplane camera on my knees and arranged additional equipment and a couple of spare cameras, telephoto lenses, and some aerial filters on the low shelf behind my shoulders. The space was so cramped, and any extra movement so pinched, with the parachute crowded on my back, that I wanted to be sure I had everything near at hand where I could reach it in a hurry. There was no room in the Cub to wear helmets, as our heads touched the roof. Someone had lent me one of the fur caps used by our Alaska troops, and I tucked my hair back under it and tied it firmly around my chin. When you lean out into the slipstream with an airplane camera, any escaping strand of hair will lash into your eyes and sometimes blind you during just that vital second when you are trying to catch a picture. The Captain lowered the whole right side of the airplane, folding it completely out of the way so I would have an unobstructed area in which to lean out and work. Then he spoke into his microphone. "Mike-Uncle-Charlie! This is Mike-Uncle-Charlie five-zero. I'm taking off on a mission. Stand by!"

"Who is Mike-Uncle-Charlie?" I asked.

"That's our brigade HQ's code word for today," replied the Captain. "Just our phonetic alphabet for MUC—today's call letters. When I find something that radio guy will be sitting up there with his ear phones on, listening."

The ground crew spun the props. "We'll be back in time for lunch," shouted Captain Marinelli to Lieutenant Strok as we started to taxi between the shell craters. I glanced at my watch, which registered quarter after eleven, and couldn't help wondering if we really would be back for lunch. I was trying hard not to wonder whether we would be back at all.

As we headed toward the front I was impressed with how regular the pattern of war, seemingly so chaotic from the ground, appears from the air. The tracks of pattern bombing on an airfield were as regular as though drawn with ruler and compass. In some olive groves the traffic patterns made by trucks and jeeps which had parked there looked as if a school child had drawn circles in a penmanship exercise, his pen filled not with ink but with a silvery mud-and-water mixture which held the light of the sun. Each bridge had been demolished with a Teutonic precision. The delicate arches of the small bridges were broken through the crest; larger bridges were buckled like giant accordions. Paralleling these were bypasses and emergency bridges which our engineers had thrown up. Most regular of all was German railroad demolition. Between the rails an endless succession of V's marched into the distance, an effect produced by the giant plow which the retreating Germans had dragged from their last railroad train, cracking each tie in two so neatly that it seemed as if someone had unrolled a narrow length of English tweed, flinging this herringbone strip over the hills and valleys of Italy.

The irregularities were furnished by the smashed towns, so wrecked that seldom did two walls stand together, and never was a roof intact.

Flying low, sometimes we could see Italian civilians picking through the sickening rubble that once had been their homes.

As we flew over the ghastly wreckage of Mignano and headed toward the still more thoroughly wrecked town of San Pietro, suddenly our plane was jarred so violently that it bounced over on its side, and we heard what sounded like a thunderclap just below.

"That's a shell leaving one of our big hows," Marinelli said as he righted the plane.

"Sounded close," I said.

"I'd hate to tell you how close," Captain Marinelli replied.

"How are you going to know when you get to the front?" I asked.

"Oh, that's easy," he explained. "When you stop seeing stars on things you know you've left your own side behind."

I looked down and saw our jeeps, trucks, and half-tracks crawling along Highway Six below us, each plainly marked with its white star.

"But the best way to tell is by the bridges," he continued. "As long as you see trestle bridges below you know we're over friendly territory, because those are bridges our engineers have built. When you begin spotting blown-out bridges you know we're approaching no man's land. The last thing the Germans do when they pull out is to blow up their bridges, and if they haven't been repaired it's because it's been too hot for our men to get in and mend them.

"When you see a stretch of road with no traffic at all, that's no man's land. And when you see the first bridge intact on the other side, you know you're crossing into Jerry territory."

We were flying over the crest of hills which surrounded Cassino valley like the rim of a cup. Highway Six wound between bald, rocky mountains here, and we almost scraped their razorback edges as we flew over. I could look down and see entrenchments and gun emplacements set in layers of rock. Then the land dropped away sharply, and all at once we were high over Cassino corridor.

As I looked down, the earth seemed to be covered with glistening polka dots—almost as though someone had taken a bolt of gray coin-spotted satin and unrolled it over the landscape. I knew these were shell holes, thousands of them, and made by the guns of both sides, first when we shelled the Germans here, and now by their guns shelling us. As we rose higher I could look down and see hundreds of thousands of these holes filled with rain and glistening in the sun.

"It's been so rough down there," said Captain Marinelli, "that the boys are calling it Purple Heart Valley."

I could hardly believe that so many shells could have fallen in a single valley. It was cruelly contradictory that with all this evidence of bloodshed and destruction, the valley seemed to clothe itself in a sequin-dotted gown.

As we flew on, we glanced back toward our own territory and could see the muzzle flashes from our guns winking on and off as though people were lighting matches over the hillsides. Each gun flash left a smoke trail until our Allied-held hills appeared to be covered with the smoke of countless campfires.

"The worst of that smoke is from our howitzers," Marinelli said.

And then he added, "Usually we don't fly across the lines unless the mission absolutely requires it. But it looks to me as though we're going to have to today, to find that *Nebelwerfer*. O.K. with you?"

"I'm right with you, Captain."

We circled lower over a loop of Highway Six where wrecked tanks were tumbled around the curve of road. "First day they've brought tanks out into the open," said Marinelli. "I want to radio back a report." The tanks seemed to have been picked off one by one as they tried to round the bend, but I could see one tank charging bravely ahead. Then as we bobbed over it, I could see a giant retriever coming in with a derrick to evacuate one of the blasted tanks.

Just beyond we began seeing demolished bridges, and we circled above these also, because the Captain's secondary mission was to report on any bridges that had been blown up. He was just phoning back his observations, and I was taking pictures, when suddenly our plane was rocked sharply back and forth and we heard a sound like freight trains rumbling under us.

"Jerry shells," said Marinelli. "High explosives! You know, they've been missing that road junction by a hundred yards every day this week."

We were tossing around violently now, and dark whorls and spirals of greasy smoke were blanketing the ground beneath.

"We've got infantry troops down there," the Captain said. The realization was almost more than I could bear—that our own boys were trying to slog through that fatal square of earth being chewed up by high-explosive shells.

An instant later we were flying over a desolate stretch of road with no traffic at all. This, then, was no man's land. At the farther end we saw a beautifully arched ancient bridge, its masonry quite intact.

"Jerry territory," said the Captain, and took the plane sharply upward.

Over our own side the Cubs make a practice of flying low, because this makes an attack by enemy fighters more difficult, as they cannot come in under; but when the observation planes cross the lines, they must increase altitude, for without armor they are very vulnerable to small-arms fire.

In search of the German rocket gun, we flew four miles over enemy territory and Captain Marinelli began hunting for the *Nebelwerfer* in the region of San Angelo.

"That's the 'Gargling River,'" he pointed out. "GI for Garigliano. And there's the Rapido." The road to Rome stretched forward into the distance, with a railroad running parallel some distance to the left. A hairpin turn branched upward toward the Benedictine monastery, at that time still intact. The ruins of Cassino lay in white smudges at the foot of snowcapped Mt. Cairo.

Cassino corridor presented an extraordinary appearance, with white plumes rising up at intervals from the valley floor. These were phosphorus shells from our own Long Toms, falling on the enemy. Whenever one landed close below us we could see it opening out into a pointed splash of fire, which quickly became transformed into a rising chunk of smoke.

Suddenly I spotted a tiny silhouette in the sky, behind us. "There's a plane," I yelled.

"Just another Cub out on a mission," said Marinelli. "But you did the right thing. Tell me anything you see."

Just then he picked up the flash of the German *Nebelwerfer*—too quick for my untrained eye—and caught sight of the shrubbery blowing back on the ground from the gun blast.

"Mike-Uncle-Charlie," he spoke into his microphone. "This is Mike-Uncle-Charlie five-zero. Enemy gun battery located at co-ordinate 86-16-2. I can observe. Over."

Then to me, over his shoulder, "It's going to take them a little time now, because they've got to compute their data and consult their fire-direction chart to see which guns can reach the target. They'll let me

Lieutenant Michael Strok (Captain now) flew me all over the front. He is a superb and inventive pilot, comes from Ithaca, New York, and Cornell. "One Cub in one day can call down more destruction than a squadron of Flying Fortresses."

PHOTOGRAPH SECTION I. FLIGHT OVER PURPLE HEART VALLEY

Below us lay the Volturno and ahead stood the mountain barrier, heavy with the menace of German guns. The Cub's job was to hunt them out, and direct with accuracy the fire of our artillery.

"You can come along if you want to . . ." Captain Jack Marinelli, of Ottumwa, Iowa, was on his way up to locate a German rocket gun.

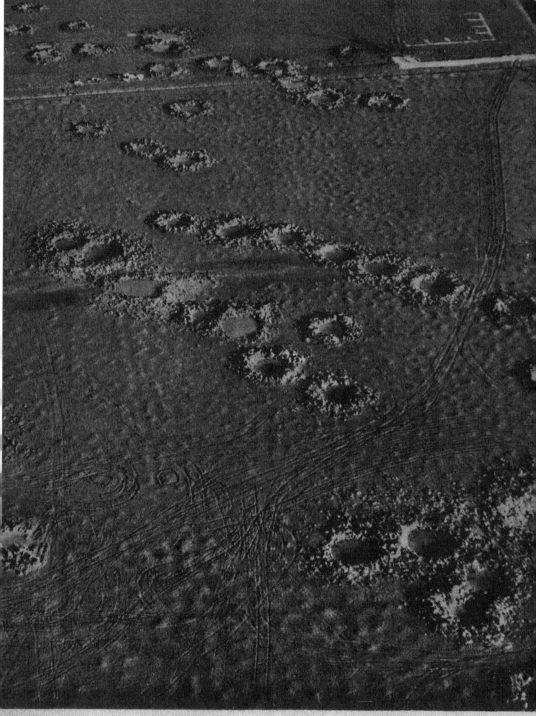

Wherever we flew we found the face of Italy scarred like the face of the moon.
This airfield shows the pattern.

Below us, always, the tracks of war. Moving in mud, tanks, heavy trucks, artillery could not conceal their footprints.

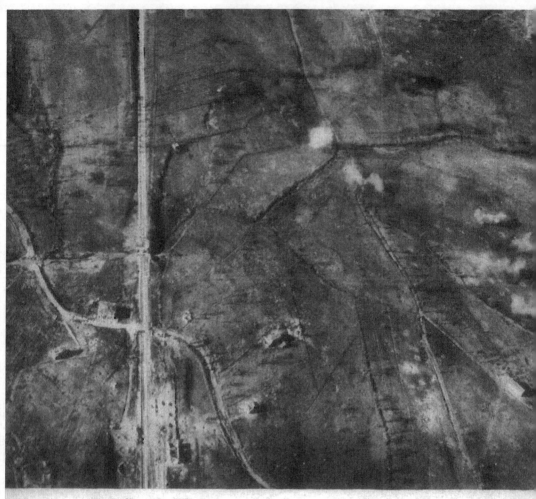

Marinelli said: "That's no man's land down there. They're shelling our troops just below." It was still too hot for us to rebuild the bridges.

Many men will remember the Rapido River as long as they live. Here it lay below us. Thousands of shell holes pock the valley, turning their stagnant, water-filled faces to the sky. From the air a shell hole made by a German gun looks just like one made by an American gun.

Marinelli said: "Range O.K. Deflection O.K. Fire for effect." We could look down and see the square blanketed with fire.

The rocket gun was washed out. Our artillery was deadly and accurate, as Germans on Highway Six that day knew.

Italian villages which died in Purple Heart Valley.

Highway Six, disappearing into the distance, was the road to Rome. At the foot of snow-capped Mt. Cairo was Cassino. Above the town we could see the ancient Benedictine monastery from which the Germans were watching the Americans come up to the valley.

The white puff (just left of highway) is a phosphorus shell fired when the Cub pilot
radioed back his findings.

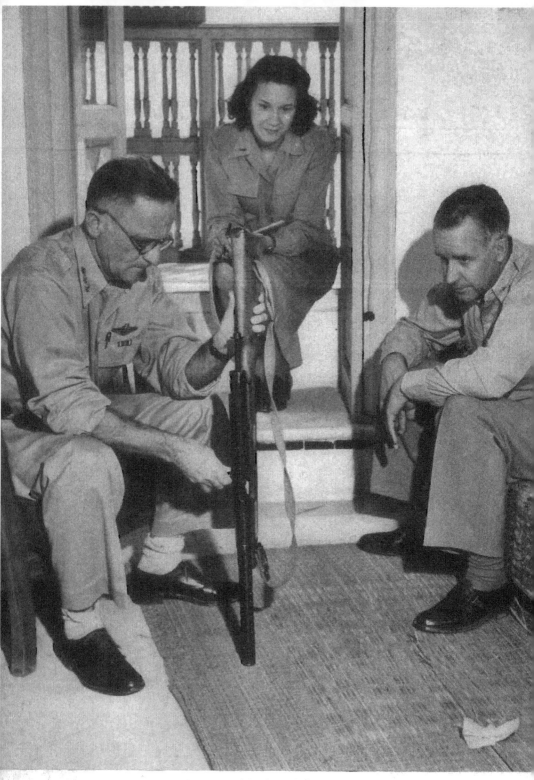

This is really a picture of Captain Sally Bagby, first WAC to be aide to a general. Her chief, Lt. Gen. Carl A. Spaatz, looks at a captured Italian automatic rifle while his chief of staff, Brig. Gen. Edward P. Curtis, watches. Captain Bagby comes from New Haven, Missouri, and has five brothers in the army. Sally was entrusted with as many important secrets as any other officer in Italy.

"Uncle Joe" Cannon is the major general who commands the Twelfth American Air Force. He is bandaged after "ditching" a smoking P-51 in the Mediterranean—the only pilot who has ever managed this successfully. The WAC is Captain Bagby.

With a French ambulance driver is Brigadier General Theodore Roosevelt, who had been wounded five times in combat, died at the front.

When you see the great machines of war and the small tools which fit a man's hand, the medicines which succor a soldier in necessity, you should remember someone has had to find the tools and get them there on the spot. Lieutenant General Brehon Somervell, chief of the Army Service Forces, is the man.

know when they've assigned a battery. We'll be hanging right around here, so speak up if you want to be put into position for anything special."

There were many things that I wanted to be put into position for. Below us it looked as though someone were shaking an enormous popcorn shaker with white grains of popcorn bursting all over the valley floor. These were thickest in front of Cassino. The Captain maneuvered the plane so that I was practically lying on my side over the valley, and—strapped in safely—I could get an unobstructed view of the battleground below.

In a few minutes a message came through that Xray-King-Item would fire. While I took pictures of the popcorn-sprinkled valley, Marinelli carried on his radio conversation with Xray-King-Item, the battery assigned to knock out the *Nebelwerfer*.

I was overwhelmed to learn that it would be my pilot, up in our little Cub, who would actually give the command to fire. The next message he received was, "Mike-Uncle-Charlie five-zero, this is Xray-King-Item. Will fire on your command. Over."

"Fire," said Marinelli, and the reply came back, "Seventy-two seconds. On the way."

It seemed amazing that the shell traveling from the Long Tom battery several miles back of us would take almost a minute and a quarter to reach the enemy gun target below. The Captain was checking with his watch. "Don't want to sense the wrong round," he explained.

He had to make this precise time check because with other guns peppering the valley it was easy to make an error, and it would have caused great confusion had he started correcting the aim of some other gun.

On the seventy-second second, a white geyser began rising toward us from below, and we knew that this was Xray-King-Item's smoke shell. Marinelli spoke into his microphone: "Xray-King-Item; this is Mike-Uncle-Charlie five-zero; five hundred yards right, one hundred yards short. Over."

Then he explained, "We've got to give them a little time again to make their correction. They're laying number-one gun on it now. When they get it adjusted they'll tie in the whole battery."

Soon another message came from Xray-King-Item: seventy-two seconds on the way. Again at the end of seventy-two seconds a feather of smoke rose from below. The aim was closer now: "Five-zero right; seven-zero short," Captain Marinelli radioed.

I realized that the Captain was handling a great many tasks at once. Not only was he checking his watch during each seventy-two-second interval, radioing his sensings in terms of deflection and elevation data, but he was keeping an eye on the sky for enemy planes. And taking care of me, too! Every time I saw a fresh shell burst I would yell to be put in position, and he would maneuver the Cub so that I could photograph while he observed.

Suddenly he exclaimed, "We're being shot at." We could hear faint sounds as though twigs were snapping against the plane—a little like hot grease spitting in a frying pan just beyond us. "It's a Spandau," said Marinelli, and he knew exactly what to do. Since the Spandau, a German machine gun, has an effective range up to 2400 feet, he simply circled up to 3200 feet, where he went on making his observations and I went on taking photographs.

"Hands cold?" he called.

They were almost numb. At our higher altitude the air was colder and I had been leaning out into the windstream with the camera. The Captain, more protected by the nose of the Cub, stripped off his gloves and gave them to me.

The whole process of adjusting fire had gone on for about fourteen minutes when Captain Marinelli finally radioed, "Deflection correct, range correct. Fire for effect."

"They're bringing in several batteries this time," said the Captain. "And this time it will be HE shells."

At the end of seventy-two seconds we could see that whole area being blanketed, not with white smoke bursts as before, but with the deadlier high-explosive shells. Curls and twists of black smoke spurted over the ground and billowed upward, and we knew that the *Nebelwerfer* was being chewed to bits.

"This is Mike-Uncle-Charlie five-zero," called Captain Marinelli. "Target area completely covered. Fire effective. Enemy battery neutralized."

Less than a minute later he exclaimed, "I see a fighter." Then, "I see two fighters."

Coming around Mt. Cevaro I could see them too: a black speck growing larger and behind it another smaller speck. In less time than it takes to tell, they had taken on the size and shape of airplanes.

We were in such a steep dive by that time that I was practically standing on my head, when I heard Marinelli say, "I see four fighters."

Sure enough, there were four shapes coming toward us, looking unmistakably like Focke-Wulf 190's.

This was the steepest dive I had ever been in in my life. I tried to take a picture, a plan I very quickly had to abandon because, with the whole side of the plane completely open, and the shelf behind me full of cameras and lenses, it was all I could do to hold back my equipment with my elbows and shoulders, to keep it from sailing into space.

I was bracing myself with the back of my neck when Captain Marinelli exclaimed, "I've lost my mike. Can you find my mike for me?" I knew he needed his microphone so he could report the fighters as a warning to all the other Cubs in the air. Groping with my left hand, and holding back my cameras with my right elbow, I retrieved his mike and handed it to him. We were still gliding down at a terrific angle when he reported, "Four enemy fighters sighted."

We were within fifteen feet of the ground when he pulled out of that dive. I have never seen such flying. He ducked into a gully and began snaking along a stream bed. Soon we were behind a small hill and over our own territory, where the fighters could not follow us in so low. In another instant we were behind a mountain and blocked from sight of the enemy planes.

We flew back to our field in time for mess, and when we rolled into the tiny landing strip, the ground crew came running up, bursting with news. To Captain Marinelli this news was much more exciting than being chased by four Focke-Wulfs: there was steak for lunch.

CHAPTER 2

Number-Three Priority

I HAD COME to Italy by air, flying by Clipper to ETOUSA and by troop transport plane to NATOUSA. ("They sound like aunts of Hiawatha," one of my friends wrote.) In the abbreviated vocabulary used by the Army, these stand respectively for European and North African Theaters of Operations, United States Army. After completing my work in NATOUSA, I was sent from MBS to PBS: from the Mediterranean Base Section to the Peninsular Base Section.

As war correspondents, we go through the same formalities as Army personnel on transfers; although we may choose our spots, subject to Army approval, we obtain orders from the office of the commanding general. Our passage is free, but it must be authorized by the military authorities to whom we are responsible.

My travel orders—number-three priority—were headed cryptically in big red letters: U.S. CONFIDENTIAL EQUALS BRITISH SECRET. This sounded very hush-hush indeed. But it was less so than if they had been marked: U.S. SECRET EQUALS BRITISH MOST SECRET. Army legend has it that the ultimate in secret documents are classified: DESTROY WITHOUT READING.

My papers may not have been MOST SECRET, but they certainly were most impressive. They were supplied to me with six carbons, and they read:

SUBJECT: Travel orders

TO: All concerned

1. Following will proceed by first available transportation from North Africa to Italy, to such places within the Theater as may be necessary for the accomplishment of her mission.

2. Travel by military aircraft is authorized. Rations in kind will be provided.

Margaret Bourke-White, Photographer

By command of General EISENHOWER.

Even traveling with all this CONFIDENTIAL EQUALS SECRET stuff, I still found myself resorting to what we correspondents call hitchhiking. You hang around an airport until something is going your way and there is room for you on it. In my case, in addition to finding space for myself, I had to find room for one Speed Graphic, two Rolleiflexes, three Linhofs, a Graflex fitted for telephoto, a battery of interchangeable lenses, various filters, film packs, flash guns, flash bulbs, a bedroll, and a typewriter.

Several months before, when a torpedoing during the North African invasion had made almost a clean sweep of my photographic equipment except for a few small odds and ends I had managed to take with me in the lifeboat, I had resolved, while still bobbing around on the high seas, that if I ever reached shore I would replace my cameras with smaller sizes. It took a torpedoing to make me really appreciate a Rolleiflex, that admirable, compact, featherweight camera. I had to comb the entire United States to replace the rest of the equipment, but I did it uniformly in $2\frac{1}{4}$x$3\frac{1}{4}$ size. I am a fanatic about interchangeability of parts. Especially in a war zone, where it is so easy to break things and so impossible to replace them, I carry duplicate cameras so I can pull out a new one when the one I am using gets out of order, and I have all my accessories and lens mounts machined so that any item will fit into any camera. Each of the three Linhofs was fitted with a range finder and infinity stops, so it could be used either on a tripod or hand-held like a Speed Graphic. All lenses, including those on the Rolleiflexes, were fitted with synchronizers for flash-bulb equipment. This arrangement proved invaluable in Italy, for it rained so much that I would have lost many daylight pictures had it not been for synchronized flashes.

The paring of my film size from the $3\frac{1}{4}$x$4\frac{1}{4}$ I had used on previous voyages to the $2\frac{1}{4}$x$3\frac{1}{4}$ size used on this trip shaved two hundred pounds off the weight of my raw film stock and supplies. All told, my seven cameras with their thirty-odd lenses, their infinite repair parts and accessories, along with sufficient quantity of film and peanut flash bulbs to last half a year, weighed 250 pounds. This was an improvement over the 450 pounds I had carried to the wars the year before, and a great reduction from the 800 pounds with which I had flown across China into Russia at the outbreak of the war with Germany. To compress my equipment and supplies into 250 pounds I had figured down to the last ounce.

My clothes fitted into the fifty-five pounds allotted airplane travelers in war zones. This poundage was not easy to achieve either, as it had to include both summer and winter uniforms, skirts for those occasions when even a war photographer has to wear a skirt, trousers to work in, heavy field clothes, boots, and woolen underwear.

What a war correspondent wears has been carefully laid down in the rule books by the War Department in Washington. A war correspondent wears officer's uniform but without officer's insignia. We have an insignia of our own which has made striking progress since the beginning of the war. First, it was a green armband (green signifies noncombatant) bearing the unfortunate letters WC. Many war correspondents were made happier when this was reduced simply to C for the reporters and P for the photographers. (Photographers in battle areas are classified as war correspondents.) Now we have replaced the wide green armbands, which were always clumsy and slipping out of place, with a neatly designed patch reading U. S. War Correspondent. In place of the usual shoulder bars worn by officers, we wear metal cutout insignia bearing the words War Correspondent, and on our caps and lapels we wear the army US. The purpose of our uniforms is not only to take on protective coloration among soldiers, but to save us from being shot as spies if we are captured. If we are taken prisoner we have another privilege in addition to staying alive. We receive pay, just as Army officers and soldiers do, under international law. Since we have no actual rank, we were given an arbitrary rank which at the beginning of the war was second lieutenant. Imagine my delight on my return to the battle zone last fall to find that we had been promoted. We are now theoretical captains. But we have to be captured before we start collecting that captain's pay, and we are always subject to certain Army regulations, and may be court-martialed.

Becoming a war correspondent is a matter of the most thorough investigation on the part of the War Department, as to background, patriotism, and reliability. By the time you are accredited you have no secrets from the War Department and neither do your ancestors; but it is right that this should be so because as a war correspondent you have access to many sources of vital military information. You are in a position of great trust.

I was a very proud girl indeed when I first received the Army credentials for which I had applied, as *Life* photographer, shortly after our country went into the war. The War Department had a new problem with me since I was a woman photographer. They had shown no dis-crimination, I am happy to say, because of my sex; the difficulty was in deciding what I should wear. They knew what the men should wear, be-cause that had been laid down in the Army handbooks, but no one had ever had to dress a woman war correspondent accredited in America. I spent five days in Washington going over materials and details with the Army War College, and finally it was decided that I should wear just what the men war correspondents wear: the same type of blouse, coat, field cap, etc., as an officer wears, but with a skirt for "dress."

I had my uniform tailored to fit me, and I loved it. Then, during the torpedoing I have mentioned, all but the clothes on my back were sunk. The losses included some prized items: a fine pair of jodhpur boots which had been made for me in London, as only Bond Street can make them, and a neat little "battle jacket" such as pilots wear. These Air Force togs had been designed by General Eaker, and he had given the original jacket model to General Spaatz, who still wears it. Mine was made by London military tailors, during the time I was accredited to the Eighth Air Force, and it was the first that had ever been made for a woman.

I was almost as distressed by having these clothes sunk as by losing my cameras. When I finally arrived like a drowned rat in Algiers, I was taken for a drying out by my Air Force pals to the gingerbread villa then occupied by General Spaatz. Inside the door the first person I ran into was General Eaker, who had flown down for a conference with "Tooey" Spaatz.

"I lost that wonderful jacket you designed," I blurted out, "and my beautiful jodhpurs."

So General Eaker, on his return to London, called up the shops, found they had my measurements on file, and a new pair of jodhpurs and a new battle jacket arrived in time for the Italian campaign.

After a torpedoing everybody helps you. General Doolittle had greeted me with the words, "Margaret, what do you need most?"

"I'd love to have another shirt to change into," I said. And then I hesitated.

"What else?" he asked.

"Well, of course I lost all my pajamas."

"Now I know why I've been carrying my sister-in-law's pajamas all these years," said kind General Jimmy. "She gave me green silk ones.

I've never used them because I always sleep raw, but if you want them, they're yours."

The pajamas were wonderful, and the shirt with which he presented me had a history. After the bombing of Tokyo, when Jimmy Doolittle landed by parachute with his men in China, and finally made his way to the outside world, he arrived in Cairo with as meager a wardrobe as the one in which I had survived the torpedoing. Since he was to be given an official banquet that night, something had to be done. He found an Egyptian tailor who promised to make a uniform in a single day. By six in the evening a uniform of sorts was completed, but the blouse was so short, reported General Jimmy, that it reached up to his chest, and the shirt was so wide that it needed tucks. It was this shirt that he gave me, and I took it to an Arab tailor on the edge of the Sahara. The Arab spoke French, so to him the shirt was *la chemise du Général.* Cut down to fit me, the Doolittle shirt did splendid service, although to the pilots with whom I worked it was always known as the General's chemise.

So in the fall of 1943, when I packed for North Africa and Italy, into my fifty-five pounds went the Doolittle shirt, my new jodhpur boots, and the new battle jacket designed by General Eaker. And at the bottom of my flight bag went one unwarlike item—an evening dress designed for me by Adrian in Hollywood. "I want something to dance in with soldiers," I had told him; adding, "if I get the chance. And it must pack up so small that it would fit in the palm of your hand."

Adrian had created just the right dress. It had a transparent white shirtwaist top and a cleverly draped black filmy skirt. Off, it was one of those little numbers that look prim on the hanger; on, there was nothing schoolteacherish about it.

As on all trips, I carried cosmetics in a little pigskin-fitted case. I think I would have gone to the battlefield without rations before I would go without face cream. I remember once when this so fascinated a certain infantry major with whom I shared a dugout during a night at the front that he nicknamed me Crisco-puss. I also carried vitamins, but I might have spared those ounces of weight, for Army food is so well planned and substantial that never once did I feel the impulse to reach for a vitamin.

Each year, when I prepare for my trip to the war fronts, the selection of which spot I am to cover is the subject of much attempted crystal-gazing among the editors of *Life* and myself. We get together and discuss how we think the news may develop and what places I am most interested in covering. The final choice is a mutual one. I always want to get to the spot where we think there will be the biggest news, and this is just where they want me to be to take photographs.

So far our guesses have been good ones, although none of us profess to be prophets. Much credit for the selections goes to Mr. Wilson Hicks, *Life*'s executive editor, formerly of AP, who seems to have an almost instinctive sense for how the news will unfold.

In the spring of 1941, both my executive editor and I believed that Russia would soon be big news. Only a month after I arrived there Germany invaded the Soviet Union, and I was fortunately on the spot to photograph the Russian war. In the summer of 1942, before a single Flying Fortress had flown over enemy territory, Mr. Hicks foresaw that the growth of our Bomber Command would be one of the great stories of the war. This was a happy choice, for I love airplanes. I became accredited to the Air Force, working with our heavy bombers during those early history-making flights from England, and following through with the North African campaign.

So in the summer of 1943, my editor and I again brought out the crystal ball and did our guessing about how we thought events might develop.

"I'd like to see the war on the ground," I said. "I'd like to photograph artillery. And see what the Engineers are doing. And there must be dozens of things that go on to make up a war that our American public doesn't know much about."

Just at this time an inquiry came for my services from the Army Service Forces in the War Department. Under General Brehon Somervell, the ASF was doing a gigantic job of supply about which our American people knew little. Sixty per cent of the war was a matter of supplying our troops with food, ammunition, medical and even spiritual services (the latter under chaplains). All this was the result of a chain-belt system which girdled the world—reached from our factories to the front lines, according to a process known to the Service Forces as "logistics." But to most American people "logistics," if they ever heard it, was just a word. That was where I came in. From their headquarters in the Pentagon Building, the ASF issued a request that I go overseas with our Army to show how supplies are brought to our troops: to tell in photographs the great story of "logistics."

This logistics business suited everybody. It pleased *Life,* because they could show in pictures that "it's a big war," which was the title they subsequently gave to one series of pictures I turned out during my mission. It delighted me, because it gave me a chance to follow up many of the subjects in which I was most interested. Having always liked industrial photography, I was eager to portray the Engineers. ASF in addition to Engineers and Quartermaster, includes Medical Corps, Transportation, Signal Corps, WAC's, Chaplains, and Ordnance. Through Ordnance I would reach Artillery. Through many of these diversified activities I would reach the soldier at the front and picture his activities from a new point of view. The focal point of all this gigantic system of service and supply was the front-line soldier, and that was the story that I wanted to tell in pictures.

I left by plane on Labor Day, 1943, and flew by way of England to North Africa. I carried in the pocket of my new summer uniform an informal note which brought me the world. It read:

WAR DEPARTMENT

Headquarters

Army Service Forces, Washington, D.C.

3 September 1943

Commanding General, NATOUSA
Army Service Forces

Dear Tom:

Margaret Bourke-White is coming to the North African theater to take pictures of Army Service Forces' operations; I have felt for a long time the need for such a service and was quite happy to accept her offer and that of her employer to do the job for us.

I am particularly anxious that Miss Bourke-White be given opportunity to photograph the complete supply and service story in the actual theater of war and will appreciate any assistance you and your staff can give to her.

Sincerely,

/s/ Bill

BREHON SOMERVELL
Lieutenant General
Commanding

That "in the actual theater of war" phrase was the most helpful one General Somervell could have written. It did much to overcome that natural reluctance in some quarters to allow a woman into the combat zone.

The "Tom" to whom it was written was a two-star general in NATOUSA who turned out to be someone with whom I had ridden horseback in Montana. It had been when *Life* magazine was still in the planning phase, before it had reached the newsstands, that I was sent out to cover some of our large government power projects. Major General Thomas B. Larkin, then a colonel, was in charge of construction of the Fort Peck Dam. He was helpful to me then in securing photographs which were used as the cover and lead feature for the first issue of *Life,* and he was equally helpful to me during my work in NATOUSA.

It was "Dear Tom" Two-Star who facilitated my quick passage to Italy when Naples fell. It was members of his equally helpful staff who brought Corporal Padgitt into my life.

Corporal Jess Padgitt from Des Moines was blond, neat, and twenty-one. He was a member of an infantry guard, and he was assigned to help me in my work. He looked like any nice kid from Iowa, and talked about as much as Harpo Marx. He was one of those rare souls who never had to be told anything twice. In fact, Padgitt seldom had to be told anything once. With no previous experience in photography, he noticed that I reached for articles in a certain order when taking pictures. On our second day out, he started handing me those items in that order. He observed that after each picture I wrote certain caption material. With no instructions from me, he produced a notebook and kept this data: name and home town of soldiers photographed; what jobs they held before entering the army; what jobs they wished to go into after the war.

It used to amuse me to see the way he had even adopted my wording: "Do you mind telling your age?" or "Are you married, engaged, or in love?" Possibly once a fortnight he would drop a voluntary comment. If he particularly liked a soldier whom I photographed, I might hear him murmur, "That was a good Joe," or conversely, "What a jerk!"

Otherwise, his reactions toward the world, and his ambitions, he kept to himself, with one exception. "Gives a guy a chance to learn something," he might say, after some new experience. Or, "Hope I can learn something in this man's army that will be useful after the war."

I love people who don't talk. Especially when taking photographs.

Photography, unhappily, takes a lot of thinking about, and assistants like the Corporal, who don't interrupt you with chatter, are rare indeed. So we did our work in mutual near-silence for several weeks before I found out what he wanted to learn to "be useful after the war."

His sole aim in life, the lodestar toward which he pointed, was law. Somehow the Corporal had come into possession of a legal tome as heavy as man's head. It was the *Army Manual of Courts-Martial*, published for the Judge Advocate General's office, and contained documents, processes, and decisions of a legal nature. It was evidently love at first sight between the Corporal and the Judge Advocate General's manual. By the time I made Padgitt's acquaintance he had practically committed it to memory, and during our subsequent travels through wartorn Italy this volume never left him.

When he was assigned to be my man Friday, he was voicelessly overjoyed to be rescued from what had been a rather monotonous job as guard before the front door of AFHQ. It gave him "a chance to learn something." And when my flying orders came through to go to Italy, he was in a silent agony of fear that he would be left behind. However, when my last lens and flash bulb were packed, the Army moved in its mysterious way. Between AFHQ and NATOUSA, and possibly "Dear Tom" Two-Star for all I know, Padgitt's U.S. CONFIDENTIAL EQUALS BRITISH SECRET orders suddenly came through.

The Corporal's orders were only slightly more detailed than mine. They began:

> Following will proceed from this station to Italy on temporary duty in order to carry out the instructions of the Commander-in-Chief, and upon completion of mission return to proper station.

He also was to receive "rations in kind."

There were no details about the "instructions of the Commander-in-Chief." I, evidently, was the lucky personification of his "temporary duty."

"This really is keen," was Padgitt's comment.

We were loading the equipment into the jeep for the airport when another powerful document came through from headquarters. This bore no CONFIDENTIAL or SECRET labels. With it was provided a handful of "certified true copies" which I was entitled to show to any interested party, in quarters where it might have beneficent results. It was from another Two-Star, the Deputy Theater Commander and commanding general of NATOUSA.

This glittering document read:

> The bearer of this letter, Miss Margaret Bourke-White, has been specially assigned by the War Department for the particular purpose of preparing a photographic record of the activities of the supply and other services.
>
> Miss Bourke-White's reputation as a photographer more than justifies a request on my part that she be given every facility and every opportunity for viewing and photographing activities relating to supply, maintenance, and hospitalization of the American Army.
>
> Miss Bourke-White should be permitted to take pictures of any activities without regard to censorship, which will be exercised by proper authorities at the completion of her mission.
>
> Please provide Miss Bourke-White with any necessary air or ground transportation in order that her mission may be accomplished as promptly as practicable.
>
> /s/ Major General, USA
> Deputy Theater Commander

"What are we waiting for?" said Padgitt, and we jumped into the jeep and drove out to the airport.

At Maison La Blanche, the airdrome, we found there was room for only one in a bucket-seat job bound for Tunis. The El Ouina airfield at Tunis was a good bet for making connections to Sicily or Italy, and I flew on to try my luck there. Padgitt would follow as quickly as he could get the breaks.

When our plane circled over Tunis Bay and prepared to land at El Ouina, I could hardly believe that we wouldn't be shot at. During the North African campaign I had been permitted by General Doolittle to go along on a bombing mission and to photograph the raid from the lead plane of our formation of Flying Fortresses. The El Ouina airfield had been our target, and from a height of six miles our planes had dropped their loads, setting such huge fires among the enemy planes massed on the field below that columns of smoke had risen thousands of feet into the air. Enemy ack-ack batteries had opened up at us, and we had been chased homeward by Messerschmitts.

But today the lovely Tunis harbor and the fine El Ouina airfield were in Allied hands. When we came in for a landing, we rolled down a runway still bordered with the twisted wrecks of the planes I had photographed burning during our bomb run. Across the road was a German graveyard, dotted with the wooden swastikas which the Germans use instead of crosses. Ninety per cent of them bore the same date: January 22—the date of the raid I had photographed during the war for Tunisia.

While I waited for transportation in Tunis, I again stayed at the Villa Spaatz. This had even more gingerbread than the one requisitioned for him in Algiers. It was done completely in lattice-carved marble. The ground floor was bisected through its entire length by a sort of alabaster ditch, intended, I suppose, for goldfish, but useful only in tripping up all of us during blackout and getting everybody's feet wet.

"Tooey" Spaatz is the most modest and lovable of generals; he still looked unprepossessing even against this fabulous background. At the foot of a cliff below the villa lapped the sapphire Mediterranean. Someone had given General "Tooey" an amphibious jeep, from which we could all go swimming. It would be hard to decide whether General Spaatz looked more incongruous happily puttering around in the Mediterranean at the wheel of his amphibious jeep, while the various generals in his official family splashed in the water around him, or whether he made a more remarkable picture against the alabaster and gold-leaf background of his villa.

All business at Villa Spaatz, whether it had to do with housekeeping or the Air Force, passed through the able hands of pretty, black-haired Sally Bagby. Sally was a WAC and had one of the most interesting jobs in the Army. She had come into the General's service as a secretary and had shown such intelligence and reliability that he had made her his aide. During my brief stay, she was raised from lieutenant to captain, a promotion which made all of us very happy, for Sally was considered perfect by everyone. Sally did everything, from being hostess to the many transient house guests, of which I was one, to keeping the General's poker scores. In addition, she knew more about each forthcoming campaign than most of the generals knew. The one drawback to this unique job (Captain Bagby was the first woman to be made a general's aide) was that except when she traveled with the General, she was a virtual prisoner in the villa. The information she possessed was so vital that she was not allowed to leave the house, even to go swimming.

Several times each day I went to the airfield and scattered the carbon copies of my CONFIDENTIAL EQUALS SECRET travel orders about where I thought they would do the most good. Finally one of them took, and with no time even to say "thank you" to General Spaatz for his hospitality, I was squeezed into the fuselage of a B-17 between two airplane motors which were being flown to Foggia for replacements. The presence of these engines was a fortunate thing for me, because they were so heavy that no one paid any attention to the additional weight of seven cameras and all the rest of my gear.

From Foggia to Naples there was so much traffic that hitchhiking was easy. It was more difficult in Naples to find myself a room. Most of the fine water-front hotels had been blown up either by our bombing or by German demolition. I finally got a room on the top floor of a hotel which was still intact on the summit of one of Naples' highest hills. The view from my bedroom was one of the "See-Naples-and-die" variety; which is the way I usually felt when I got there, because to reach it I had to climb five flights of stairs.

For three weeks I went around photographing the reconstruction of the harbor and the ruins of the city. Then one day in one of the main city squares, working with my head under a camera cloth, I was just reaching for a lens hood when it was passed conveniently into my hand. Next I groped for a filter, and a hand passed it into my fumbling fingers. The picture was ready now, and as I reached for a film-pack holder, it was slipped into its place in the camera. Only after the photograph was taken did I realize that the preceding steps had been a bit unusual.

I looked behind me and there stood the only person it could have been: Corporal Padgitt. "So you made it," I said.

"I slept on a bench at that airport," he said, "except one night when I got into a six-by-six to get out of the wind; but I woke up when they started to drive the truck away with me in it. When I couldn't get into a troop transport, I even tried to hitchhike piggyback on a P-38. Finally, after I was just going to write my congressman about getting another bench, on account of the one I was on had wore clear through, there was a C-54 due to take off, with room for just one more passenger. It was between me and a captain. Seeing as we both had number-three priorities, I sneaked my barracks bag on the plane while they was gassing up. When the plane was ready for the take-off they started to bounce me for the captain. But my barracks bag was under so many sacks of mail by that time that I stuck."

It was weeks before I heard Corporal Padgitt utter another speech as long as this one: not until after we had been bombed, strafed, and repeatedly shelled together.

CHAPTER 3

Nothing Ever Happens in Naples

ENGINEERING HISTORY was made in Naples Harbor. When Allied armies arrived they faced one of the most fantastic jobs of demolition the world had ever seen. This colossal destruction had been started by our own forces, bombing the enemy-held seaport; it had been completed by the Germans before they withdrew. The harbor had to be rebuilt again by us for our troops to advance. It was an unintentional partnership entered into by both sides, which produced the greatest tangle of blown-up docks, smashed warehouses, sunken ships, and snarled loading gear that American GI's and bulldozers had ever had to deal with.

Our bombers were responsible only for the broad pattern of destruction. The picture was filled in by the enemy with diabolical artistry. It was not sufficient for the retreating Germans to sink all ships that Allied air raids had left afloat. They sank them scientifically, placing each sunken ship where it would have the greatest nuisance value. Sometimes they sank one ship on top of another, chaining the two together so that the dock obstruction would be as difficult to clear as possible.

It was not enough for them to mine or dynamite all buildings lining the harbor which had escaped Allied bomb loads. Blowing them up would have made things too simple for our side. They set very carefully and delicately placed charges which blasted out only the floors and left the walls precariously standing. This made the buildings useless, but left the dangerous walls for us to level before the area was safe.

It always sounded uncanny to me when I listened to American engineers speak almost admiringly of the "beautiful job of demolition" done by the Germans, but this was an expression I was to hear often during my work on Naples Harbor. The science of demolition has progressed to incredible refinements in this war. No doubt the enemy mixed imagination with destruction, but our American engineers used just as much if not more imagination in their task of reconstruction. Many of their new devices and new tools will not be made known until after the war.

Each time a power shovel pushed over a tottering wall, as a child might push down blocks, the wreckage was put to immediate use in filling up gaps and potholes in the harbor. It was always interesting to me that we could use the rubble directly from a bombed building on the water front—load it into a dump truck, take it a few yards away, pour it into the quayside, and continue construction, basing it on a bed of destruction.

Sunken ships were ingeniously put back to work. Exposed hulls were fitted with rails and runways so they could be used in unloading troops. Bombed ships blocking the docks were simply leveled off, their smokestacks and superstructures cut away, and then reinforced to be used for docks themselves. Oil tankers clogging the harbor were bridged with prefabricated metal parts and employed as piers for unloading Liberty ships.

And over this reconstructed destruction of war, a never-ending stream of C rations, ammunition, GI boots, blankets, tentage, jeeps, bake ovens, delousing units, and blood plasma was being unloaded and rushed frontward.

Some of the most dramatic work in the harbor was invisible. Under the surface of the water divers bit away with cutting tools at the snarled debris, dismembered sunken wreckage which blocked the fairways, blasted the obstructions with which the retreating enemy had hoped to interrupt our vital stream of supplies.

I drove along the quayside with Corporal Padgitt in the jeep one day, just in time to see a waterspout go shooting into the air. It was from a heavy charge set to blast away at a sunken drydock. Immediately afterward a curlyheaded lad with an engaging grin was helped into his heavy diving helmet, and I caught his picture as he was eased down into the water.

"Oh, we didn't have time to get his name and his home town for captions," I said.

"That's Salvatore Benelli," volunteered the tender, "but you can talk to him yourself." And the boys helped me jump out to a little bobbing platform that was virtually a floating telephone booth.

"What's your home town?" I shouted into the mouthpiece.

"Long Island City," came a muffled voice from far below. "Will my picture be in all the New York papers?"

"*Life* magazine," I answered. "And maybe a book."

"Boy! This is a great day in my life," came the voice.

"How old are you?" I yelled.

"Twenty. Hey, lady, do I get a Hollywood contract out of this?"

And then, "Take a picture of my buddy from the Bronx. That tender, Ray Butler. He's a good man to have on top when you're down on the bottom."

So while Salvatore worked away on the Mediterranean floor, I photographed and talked with Corporal Butler and with Private Patsy Desarro, and Padgitt entered their names, ages, and home towns faithfully in his neat notebook.

Most of their group of twenty-three, including fifteen divers and eight tenders, had previously worked on the salvage of the *Normandie*. I discovered that diving is a proud profession with family traditions. Many of these divers were the brothers, cousins, or sons of divers.

"How do you like it here?" I asked.

"It's sure swell to see Naples," said Patsy Desarro. "My folks always talked about Napoli."

"It would be a great thing to have a beautiful girl under a full moon on the blue Mediterranean," said the boy from the Bronx. "Doesn't that sound romantic?"

"It is," said Patsy Desarro. "I know. But I had a little company. You guessed it—her mother."

"When we went into this man's army," one of the divers told me, "we were just dying to get back into diving dress again. We sure were happy when they gave us Naples Harbor to splash around in."

"The minute I got my suit wet," said another diver, "I knew I was back where I belonged."

Sergeant Benelli was bubbling to the surface by this time; when the boys had lifted off his helmet he joined in the conversation.

"I thought for a while it would be nice to try to get to wear a pair of those silver wings they talk so much about. But I couldn't picture myself in an airplane when I've been going just the opposite direction from up for such a long time.

"Then the Army had me on paper work till they thought better of it. Imagine sitting at one of those damn machines—I think they call it a typewriter—with the paw I've got. How is a guy going to punch the right key when there are fifty to choose from. Lord, what a beating that machine took! If it ever came to life, I'd have been held on an assault-and-battery charge. Anyway, I like diving too much to do anything else," he concluded.

A number of the divers who came from Italian families had relatives whom they were hoping soon to see, as our front moved forward. The Benellis came from Milano. "I've written to my mom for Grandma's address," said Salvatore. "It would be a great surprise to see one of her grandchildren."

I learned that just as pilots get flying pay, these divers received diving pay, at the rate of five dollars per underwater hour. "I'm sending my diving pay to my mom for a fur coat I promised her for Christmas," said Salvatore. "When I get home, her and I are going stepping, and I want her to look the best in the world because that is what she deserves."

It was one set of wits against another when it came to neutralizing mines in Naples. The Germans were increasing in subtlety with each new region they left behind. Early in the Italian campaign, some American boys entering the courthouse of a small town saw a picture of Hitler on the wall. It was a natural action for one of them to snatch it off the wall. He was instantly killed and his companions were maimed by a mine wired to the picture frame. Another group found a piano in a house, and one of the boys sat down to play. As soon as he touched the keys all the soldiers in the room were killed.

There were four types of booby traps, those touched off by pressure, by release of pressure, or by pull, and the chemical-mechanical type. Experts found all four as they combed through Naples buildings. Any building left fairly intact was in itself suspect and had to be elaborately checked. Every doorknob, chair, and floorboard had to be tested. With all this care, an occasional time bomb inevitably escaped detection, as in the case of the Naples post office which blew up in a sector where there were many Army offices.

A week after the post-office disaster, one or my friends, an American infantry major, had his life saved by a prostitute. He was walking through the Santa Lucia district, passing the row of once fashionable hotels lining the water front. He was about to walk into one of them, when a streetwalker accosted him. He noticed her wistful face and how starved she looked. Instead of brushing past her, as he would ordinarily have done, he paused and declined her courteously in the few words of Italian he knew. He had just started on, when the whole pavement seemed to rush up toward him. Before his eyes, the hotel folded, floor after floor, like a giant accordion, and the concussion threw him into the middle of the street. His footbones were fractured, but that brief stop on 'the sidewalk had saved his life.

It was almost a month before engineers dared to turn on the electricity in the city. Meanwhile, people had been without light, and without water, too, because the Germans had blown up the water pipes and they had to be repaired.

The engineers had to be certain that as thorough a job of mine clearance as possible had been done before turning on the electricity. There was danger that when the main switch was thrown, any number of hidden mines or time bombs might be activated and more buildings blown up.

Before the light was going to be turned on, the city had been ordered evacuated except by MP's, fire-fighting squads, and medical personnel. A radio truck had toured the city the day before, warning civilians to take to the hills. From early morning on, a flood of ragged Italians carrying chairs, food, and babies on their shoulders had swept toward the hills.

The power was to be switched on at noon. There were small knots of officers in front of each building, because it was going to be the job of each little group of soldiers and officers to go in after the main switch had been thrown and turn on one light after another. I did a lot of planning to decide where to be at the crucial moment. Padgitt and I toured the city in the jeep and consulted with the engineers as to which were the most suspected blocks of buildings. Finally we picked a spot near the Aquarium on Via Caracciolo, where we could face several streets, principally Riviera di Chiaia and Via Partenope, where occasional groups of comparatively intact buildings were considered particularly suspicious. I had a whole battery of cameras, each fitted with a different focal lens, set and ready in the jeep so we could rush to any part of the city which might start to blow.

' I remember how the same major who had been saved the week before by the streetwalker limped into his headquarters with two of his men. Turning on the light switches was a dangerous job, and he didn't want to send his men anywhere he would not go first.

The headquarters was in an old apartment house requisitioned from a countess. It would have taken only a small mine to send her paneled walls and marble stairways toppling down. I felt like a ghoul with my camera focused on the building which, if it blew, would make a fine photograph but would spell the end of the major and his men.

The power went on. One after another, lights appeared in the countess' apartment, in the naval and Air Force headquarters down the street, in the British officers' mess, in the whole row of buildings along Santa Lucia, in the buildings on the hills rising above Naples Harbor. Everything was lighted up—and not a building was blown. The entire city blazing at once was testimony to the thoroughness with which our engineers had done their job. There would be need for watchfulness for another twenty days, because chemical bombs activated by the power would still have to be guarded against. But, with care, the city would be safe. The civilians flowed back again into Naples with their chairs, their bedrolls, and their babies.

For German pilots raiding Naples, Mt. Vesuvius acted as a direction finder. Only a few carefully guarded lights were used in the harbor for the unloading of ships which went on all through the night, but these could be thrown from a single switch when German bombers approached. Nothing could be done to black out the volcano which hung like a red star above the city. All the Germans needed to do was triangulate against it.

We always knew when the Germans were coming because their nocturnal visits were heralded by an invisible visitor whom we called, inappropriately, "Cheesecake Charley"—also known as "Foto Freddie." He flew in at a relatively safe height. We knew he was circling around the harbor, taking photographs, when our ack-ack guns shot up a few warning bursts to keep him from coming in lower to get better photographs.

His mission was to make sure there was enough shipping going on in our harbor to justify a raid, and there always was because the harbor was humming by that time. As the patchwork on the quayside continued, each day saw more ships anchored against improvised piers.

Like schools of water beetles, the amphibious trucks we called "ducks" swarmed out to Liberty ships, churned back filled with "ammo," rolled up out of the water, and took to the roads. Then came the unloading of troops, and the Germans were after our soldiers as well as our shipping.

The raid would come with complete regularity at ten minutes after six, the apparent reason being that the Germans had to take off with their heavy bomb loads from their fields while there was still daylight. Therefore they couldn't fool us by occasionally coming later.

In some uncanny way, they seemed to know just when our harbor would be fullest of ships, and we always wondered how much of the information was supplied by Cheesecake Charley and how much of it might come from espionage.

I remember one night when I was photographing a raid from the window of an old building opposite the Santa Lucia Castle. The Germans were dropping multicolored flares from above, and tracers rose from ack-ack batteries ringing the shore and spotted along the upper defense range of the city. Suddenly the whole harbor came alive and every warship started shooting tracer shells toward the raiders. When a bomb fell so close that a blast of air threw me to my knees and plaster began tumbling around my head, I decided that it was time to get out of the rickety old apartment.

I got into a jeep and was driving toward the harbor just as a dive bomber scored a direct hit on an ammunition ship anchored near the dock. The explosion set fire to a large Quartermaster warehouse at the edge of the pier. Our Army fire department immediately rushed out and started fighting the fire, desperately attempting to beat out the flames.

As our soldiers fought their way through the flaming ruins, light ammunition in the warehouse began exploding in their faces. None of our men were killed. The next morning one soldier believed lost was found in a sandpile—still alive. Two members of a gun crew on an ack-ack position were dive-bombed and blown into the sea, but they managed to swim back to the shore. A girder from the warehouse flew 300 yards and fell in a stack of 100-pound bombs which were smashed and broken. Miraculously they didn't explode, or an entire section of the harbor would have been completely wiped out.

The fire fighters drew water right out of the sea, and in the course of several hours fifteen million gallons of water were pumped out of the Mediterranean and hosed onto the warehouse. By morning, colored soldiers, members of the Quartermaster Corps, were dashing into the swirling smoke and flames and emerging like Christmas trees, their necks strung with GI boots, their arms filled with tent pegs, leggings, socks, and long-handled underwear.

It was six days before the last flames were extinguished. For many long weeks our troops in the mud and rain of the Italian mountains felt the lack of clothing and tentage lost during that bomb raid.

On my way home the next morning after photographing the warehouse fire I passed through a street where a row of apartment buildings had been blasted to the ground by a direct bomb hit. Half of the last building in the block was still standing, its four complete stories laid open as though sliced from top to bottom with a giant knife. On the ceiling of the top floor and within only a few inches of the jagged break hung a perfectly preserved crystal chandelier. Three months later, when I was about to leave Naples, I passed through the same street and found that although the tons of rubble from the mashed apartment building had been cleared away, that fragment of roof still remained. The chandelier, perfect to the last glittering pendant, was sparkling in the sun.

CHAPTER 4

Life Goes Underground

ONE NIGHT during a raid over Naples, a group of guards on a hilltop hurried into an orchard for cover from dive bombers. One of the soldiers jumped into a convenient hole. When the raid was over, his companions found that he had vanished. The men lowered a soldier on a rope and kept on working him down the hole until the end of the rope was reached, after paying out fifty feet, and they had to pull him up again.

They searched until morning, when an Italian peasant led them to the bottom of the hill and took them through a crevice massed with hanging ivy. They found they were in a long subterranean passage. Finally the tunnel opened into an enormous cavern. A slender beam of daylight leaked through from a hole 150 feet above their heads. It was through this shaft that the American guard had fallen. His crushed body lay on the rocky floor.

This was no ordinary cave. It was filled with industrial machinery. The soldiers went from chamber to chamber, and everywhere they found scenes of wreckage such as none of them had ever seen before. When the Germans had had to flee from Naples they had evidently torn through these caverns, blowing up all the heavier machinery with dynamite and shooting up the more delicate equipment with pistols.

The searchers found wrecked lathes and drill presses, and smaller caves fitted up as photographic laboratories with metallurgical testing equipment for making microphotographs. One small chamber was piled to its rocky ceiling with stacks of aluminum pigs. The contents of the cave were requisitioned by a committee of Allied engineers, and the material eventually went to the British to be used for salvage.

This was the beginning of the discovery of many caves. One of the most dramatic of these was an immense series of high-arched caverns overhanging the sea and housing a complete airplane factory. For two years this plant had operated with 400 workers, 100 of whom were women. When I visited it there were still twisted frames of double-decked beds lining the walls of several caverns, where the workers had slept safe from bomb raids.

When Allied armies were drawing closer, the Germans did so thorough a job of demolition here that the rocky floors were a mass of crumpled fuselages, radio parts, propellers, and mangled bodies of aircraft. It was on September 27, when the Germans knew their days in Naples were numbered, that they set off 250 demolition bombs.

The chief engineer, Professor Raffaele Polispermi—a professor of mechanical engineering at Regia University in Naples, who had also been responsible for the design of the airplane models—managed to smuggle some of the more precious instruments out of the cavern and bury them at the bottom of the cliff. Then the professor stole to the deep recesses of one of the caverns and pulled down a lot of cabinets, so that the Germans would ignore that portion of the cavern, believing it already wrecked. He hid himself under the pile of wreckage. When they had gone on to another cave, he was able to slip out and save some of the pattern-making machinery, piling debris over it so the Germans would pass it by.

Then the Germans started pouring gasoline and benzene over the equipment, setting fire to it. Civilians had been ordered out of a strip of land 300 feet from the sea and all roads had been blocked and guarded. The professor stole through the woods to round up a few of his workmen. Twice he had to cross roads, where each time he overpowered and killed two German guards.

He and his small group of men, who had equipped themselves with blankets, made their way back to the sea wall. There they found that fire and smoke were pouring out of the mouth of the cavern. They waited until the sentry was at the far end of his beat and then, covering themselves with their blankets, which they had dipped into the sea, they ducked into the factory. They saved a complete set of the pattern- and die-making machinery, so that after the Germans moved on they were able to set up sufficient equipment to start a new factory.

During the three days of destruction by fire, a few Italians managed each night to get into the cavern for a short time. With the aid of fire extinguishers and pails of sand they contrived to save considerable material. They knew they could count on a few hours to work, for the Germans would not come into the cave because of the flames.

When I arrived to take pictures, I found an angry knot of Italian workers. They were friendly toward us but enraged at the Germans for wrecking their factory. They started begging me to put them back to work at once, not realizing that putting Italians back to work is a province over which a war correspondent has not the faintest jurisdiction.

During the transition period while this factory and others were being requisitioned by the British, the workers could not understand why there were so many delays in getting back into production. They needed their wages, for they were short of food and felt keenly the fact that their children were underfed.

This was the first of many protests about food that I was to hear on all sides from Italian civilians. And only a few days later I came upon a food riot in the streets. The people were storming a shop whose owner had been selling flour at black-market prices. I witnessed real starvation, however, the next time I ventured into a cavern.

Beginning with the first raid of Allied bombers over Nazi-held Naples in late 1942, vast numbers of Neapolitans had started moving underground. Some of them had not seen the light of day for more than a year. In one enormous cavern, originally a quarry, which had housed stores for the Italian Royal Navy, hundreds of families had assumed squatter rights. There in the dim cavernous recesses of the cliffs overhanging the city, these families gathered together the chips and scraps for a "house" and settled down to a cave dweller's existence.

Occasionally, after a heavy raid, a few of the bolder ones would steal out and rifle the bomb wreckage, coming back with perhaps a door, a bedstead, a couple of kettles, a birdcage, or even sometimes a donkey or two or three chickens. And life would go on. The more enterprising built shacks within their rocky vaults. Sometimes whole caverns took on the look of shanty towns; but the majority of the wretched inhabitants lay on piles of rags with no protection against the dampness and cold.

Never did I visit one of these caverns without being led by weak, protesting parents to the side of at least one dying child. More often there would be several in each subterranean refuge who were literally perishing from hunger.

In the face of death going on before my eyes, I felt hopelessly inadequate each time we went to photograph these caves. Crowds of children stormed around the Corporal and me, calling out what has become the familiar chant of Italian children—*caramelle, caramelle.* Padgitt and I were nearly swept off our feet each time we reached into our pockets and brought out the handfuls of hard candies we always carried. The destitution of the children seemed even more bitter to me when they laughed and shouted happily over the candies, as children always will.

It is easier to satisfy a child with a caramel than to answer some of the grownups who were frankly puzzled at the food situation.

It is not easy to administer justly an occupied city, to prevent the growth of a black market, and to see that our supplies are properly distributed. Still, our failure to do this may have serious effects on the future. I observed that the friendship with which we were greeted when we landed in Naples rapidly cooled during my stay there.

Another complication was the typhus epidemic which spread rapidly, first carried by lice and then intensified by lack of resistance caused by undernourishment. The epidemic ran unchecked for two months before corrective measures were taken. Only when it grew to frightening pro-portions in early January was something done. Then the Medical Department was called in and, with the assistance of the United States Typhus Commission, civilians were treated with lice powder and given medical care, and military personnel was quarantined from entering Naples except on urgent business.

Fortunately, we had not a single case of typhus in our Army. This is a testimony to the excellent care given our soldiers, who are superbly fed, given antityphus injections, and helped by every possible facility for cleanliness—even delousing units placed close behind the front lines.

Life in Naples had taken on some extraordinary aspects. One day I visited an old cistern where I had to go down for some hundred steps below the surface of the earth. People were living there who had made their way down those steps fourteen months before and were determined not to climb up out of the cistern until the war was over. It made little difference to them that the city was held by Americans and British instead of by Nazis. They were as terrified of the German bombs falling on us as they had previously been of Allied bombs falling on the Germans, and their resolution held firm not to show their faces to the light of day until the world was at peace.

Even the traffic tunnels which run through Naples were crowded with human beings. Our jeeps, trucks, and ducks passed in a never-ending stream along these traffic routes which connect various parts of the city, and on each side, crouched upon the sidewalk, were dozens of Italian families who had settled down to live there permanently. Sometimes they had succeeded in setting up a few boards to divide them from the family next door and to give them some slight protection against the wind which constantly swept through the tunnels. Some of the men in these families went out periodically to get work in the harbor, since many civilians were being employed there; but the women and children, wrapped in rags and crouched against the tunnel walls, had settled down to a life of lethargy.

Not only had the poor fled from Allied and German bombs, but also the rich, although, as usual, the rich were able to hide in greater comfort. High above one of the main thoroughfares of Naples rises a cliff of soft rock. A number of exquisite little modernistic houses had been chiseled out of the face of this rock, and these gave their wealthy inhabitants not only complete protection against the heaviest air raids, but also a magnificent view of one of the most spectacular harbors in Europe. Those elaborate hideaways were eventually requisitioned as American military offices.

Meanwhile, black-market prices were rising. Cargoes of wheat brought in to sell at subsistence prices to the civilians had found their way into the hands of local middlemen who were reselling them at an enormous profit. Furthermore, there were many Italian food hoarders who aggravated the problem by allowing wheat to pile up in their bins out on the farms. Our Allied armies shipped thousands of tons of supplies into Sicily and Italy, wheat and flour alone reaching a grand total, up to May 31, of 580,000 tons. In the early weeks of the occupation, when submarines were still a factor to be reckoned with, many American boys risked their lives to bring over these shiploads of food. It was unfortunate that muddled handling of supplies sometimes aggravated rather than cured the food problem. The price of flour and sugar rose to fifty and sometimes eighty cents a pound, bread to sixty cents a loaf, and soap sold for fifty cents a cake. Our Allied Military Government had done a strict job of regulating wages. Common labor received fifty lire (fifty cents) a day. Stevedores were paid eighty cents a day. The maximum pay allowed a civilian office worker or even a skilled interpreter was from sixty cents to one dollar fifty cents a day.

It was against regulations, no matter how expert the services, to pay more than that. But these wages translated into food represented a shocking discrepancy. Civilians found they had to pay three dollars a pound for ordinary cooking cheese, a commodity which had always been both cheap and common among the Italians. They had to pay ten dollars a gallon for olive oil, their own product, and a staple which had previously sold for twenty or thirty cents a gallon.

Only black-market restaurant owners could buy meat, which was soaring to a thousand lire a pound (ten dollars) on those rare days when meat was obtainable. Only the largest restaurants could purchase sacks of flour, and even then it was hard to get. When obtainable, it sold for five hundred to a thousand dollars a sack; but more often, even in black-market restaurants, a sign was placed on the tables, NO BREAD TODAY.

This condition might have been less serious if AMG had had a more clearly defined policy, but often matters got beyond them. No doubt, of course, AMG was filled with men of good will, honest and well intentioned, but theirs was not an easy problem, and in many cases, the petty brigands and thieves who profited from the sale of American food were the same Fascist profiteers who flourished before the war. However, as the months progressed, a firmer policy was adopted, and certain large black-market operators were brought into the open and placed publicly on trial; this tended to bring about improvement.

But one aspect of this problem was never clearly resolved. Under the Fascism that preceded us, a major means of getting power was to gain swift control of the courts, for if you have your own judges you can keep your thugs from being convicted. When many of these thugs continued in circulation, many anti-Fascist Italians, ready and willing to support the Allies, were in a growing frenzy of fear. In small towns as well as large cities they came to believe that when we moved on, they would be exposed again to their old enemies. This fear of vengeance placed a penalty on their co-operation with the Allies.

It seems to me that if a progressive political philosophy were made clear, much terror of the future could be spared these civilians of occupied countries. (And, incidentally, some uncertainties as to the future attitudes and actions of these civilians might be spared us also.) Among our American officers we have some honest and intelligent groups, who are doing a constructive job and deserve praise for their vision and understanding in a difficult undertaking. But the proportion of these is not high enough; too much of their good work is swamped in the general confusion.

Our aid to the Italians operates like a giant breadline, and like all breadlines has a profound effect on economy. We do not get automatic rewards for generosity unless it is employed with intelligence, and lack of intelligence is indicated by our failure to control the black market which the breadline has nurtured. If we choose to go in for breadline tactics, that breadline should be used as a sound political investment. If it is not, then a priceless opportunity will have been lost.

We Americans, moving on as a victorious army, have an opportunity to mold the world—an occasion almost unprecedented in history. Our soldiers buy that opportunity with the dearest possession they have. We have no right to ask them to lay down their lives unless we administer what they have gained with the full intelligence that their sacrifice deserves.

CHAPTER 5

Hot Spot

"JERRY'S BEEN up on that mountain looking at us down the barrels of his guns for a long time," said the engineering officer from the front of the jeep. He was on his way to a demolished road where his gang were breaking through a German-made barrier. I had been told that I might come along. With us in the jeep were Corporal Padgitt, superintending the cameras, and Captain Deutschle. Bighearted Joe Deutschle accompanied me on many of these trips. He was an ex-newspaperman, now PRO with the Army Service Forces.

"Our men have sure taken a beating on these jobs," remarked the engineer, "with the Blonds in their OP's up there hanging over each spot where we stopped to work."

We were weaving our way between the knife-edged peaks of the Colli pass, through which engineers had thrown a chain of bridges across ravines too deep for sunlight to reach. But German binoculars could probe into most of them, and enemy observers could deliberately choose which half-track, jeep, or road gang to shoot at. This was a war for high ground. The side which could see the most had the advantage. The fighting in Italy was slow and costly because for so long the enemy held the highest peaks.

The entire Fifth Army battlefield throughout the winter of 1943–44 was enclosed within a snow-tipped mountain triangle, formed by the Cassino corridor, the hills behind Venafro, and the rugged terrain backing the little town of Colli. Struggling toward the lofty edges of this triangle, soldiers and mules made their dizzy way. Running through the enclosed central area was the road to Rome, where our troops moved a few feet forward, a few inches back. Through monotonous and costly months, few but the wounded or the fallen had a chance to rest. Small wonder that in GI terminology this was Purple Heart Valley.

Today I was seeing for the first time the upper point of this triangle.

We drove over an unspectacular trestle crossing, the kind you would

A little boy in Italy is lucky when he has a father on whose shoulders he can sit and sleep.

PHOTOGRAPH SECTION II. THE WRECK OF NAPLES

The need of privacy becomes intense. With bits and ends from their wrecked home the family hoped to shut their life away from other dwellers.
Some children learn early to use tools.

Children and soldiers can always laugh.

The indestructible social unit.

Only a few could afford these modern, comfortable, bombproof cliff dwellings.

The factories went underground before the people. This one made warplanes.

Colored soldiers shared the hard work of reconditioning Naples Harbor.

Give an American engineer a bulldozer and he can do anything.

The Germans were skillful, too.
They blew up Naples Harbor just the right way to make us the most work.

Fighting is a game for specialists. Technical Sergeant Salvatore Benelli, Long Island City, Queens, was a diver before Naples Harbor needed him, and wants to go on diving after the war.

When the harbors were cleared and the LST's were loading, questions were forbidden. Anzio was in the making.

Foto Freddie came at noon, so high we could not see him. The bombers came at twilight.

After the bombers, the engineers and quartermaster troops went into action, fighting fires, salvaging stores.

The Germans, destroying a cave factory, left this tangle of cable and pipe.

Italian engineers saved some of the machinery, wanted to go on building planes. Having worked for the Germans, they found it hard to win our confidence. Naturally.

Professor Raffaele Polispermi, chief engineer of the underground airplane factory, designed the planes, claimed to have shot four Germans while trying to save the patterns.

scarcely notice if you were driving through the Poconos. "We named this 'Hot Spot Bridge,' " said the engineering officer, "because we lost eight of our engineers here last week. Really a bad break. Jerry started laying them in just five minutes before the bridge was finished."

I studied my companion's profile under his helmet. His features gave a hint of his Polish ancestry, and he had that strong-jawed resolute look which is so typically American. Lieutenant Colonel Stanley Walter Dziuban was young for his rank, only twenty-nine, and had graduated as Number One Cadet from his class at West Point. I had heard about his outstanding record with the Combat Engineers.

During the Sicilian campaign an armored car in which he was riding had struck a land mine, overturned, and caught fire. He was badly lacerated and his wrist was broken, but he was thrown free, and at the same time enemy machine-gun fire opened up on his men who were escaping from the burning car. One wounded soldier could not get free because his crushed arm was caught beneath the car. Lieutenant Colonel Dziuban ran back, amputated the man's arm with his field knife, and dragged him to safety just the instant before the car exploded. The lad he saved recovered, and Lieutenant Colonel Dziuban was awarded the Soldier's Medal.

During our journey forward I picked up a good deal of information from the engineer. I found that everybody was talking about the new mines. The Germans used to set them with time fuses which gave the discoverer, if he were quick, from two to four seconds to run a few yards and throw himself flat. Now they were often set to explode instantaneously. This gave you two choices: throw yourself flat and hope for the best, or keep one foot firmly rooted to the mine, which would cost a leg but might save some lives. I remarked that that would take incredible presence of mind.

"Some of our boys have done it," Dziuban replied, "and it protected the rest of the gang."

Then he instructed me that if I had to step off the road at any time, I should be very careful to place my feet in the footprints of someone who had gone before. Or I could walk in a jeep track, stepping right in the wheel marks. But never take a step off the road otherwise.

The German mine layers were getting craftier, he told me. They were even booby-trapping unexploded charges. And it was an old story about trapping dead bodies. Only that week a couple of his men had found a dead German soldier in the middle of this very road. They checked the body, and after ascertaining that no tripwires were attached, they lifted the dead soldier and looked around for a spot where they could give him a decent burial. A little clump of shrubs by the roadside seemed just the right place. Evidently the Germans had figured this out in advance, because although the body wasn't booby-trapped, the bushes had been. "That cost us two good engineers," the young colonel commented bitterly.

We crossed a new structural (Bailey) bridge just completed near the high-walled town of Montaquila, turned into a little rocky side road, and passed the ruins of a thoroughly demolished power plant. Retreating Germans had blown the generators off their foundations and wrecked the large aqueduct intakes along a several-hundred-foot span, making repair impossible and leaving nothing but a hillside of scrap metal and concrete.

Then around a curve of road we saw a mine-sweeping crew, clearing an area by the roadside so it could be used to park repair machinery and 'dozers. With the men advancing in couples, it looked almost like a stately dance. The sweeper went first, walking with a peculiar swinging motion, sweeping from side to side his iron pancake on its long instrument-set handle. Following close behind was his partner, carrying a rifle to protect the sweeper from snipers, and holding a tasseled marker to plant on any suspicious spot where the indicator showed buried metal.

"The demolition boys sometimes send a herd of goats in," said the engineering officer. "But up in these hills there are more mines than goats."

Just beyond the sweepers, the road shrank to a mere shelf carved into the side of the precipice. The whole riverbank here was one sheer cliff towering above us and falling to the Volturno a hundred feet below. Long ago, Italian laborers had reinforced this tortuous highway with arched abutments, but German demolition squads had made a shambles of the ancient masonry blocks. Just ahead of us the thoroughfare was completely blocked by a boulder as large and compact as a small bank building.

"The Blonds did a clever job on that one," commented Colonel Dziuban, as our jeep came to a stop. "Quite a trick to lay a charge just heavy enough to topple that big boulder over so it would come to rest right in the middle of the road."

The men had been working for two days, chipping away at the boulder with TNT charges, which they set delicately so as not to cause a landslide.

As I began focusing cameras, I took off my helmet, which kept getting in the way. "I ought to make you keep your helmet on," said Colonel Dziuban. "It's not a good idea to go around here without one. But it certainly is good to see a woman's hair again."

I think it was a few minutes before most of the road gang realized they were being photographed by a woman, because my regulation leggings, trousers, boots, and field jacket were exactly like the clothes they wore. They didn't have much to say, but they certainly gave me plenty of help.

"We're opening up the road one way only," the officer of the demolition squad explained to me. "They need to put Long Toms on that plateau just beyond. It's so rugged up here there's hardly room for your own heavy guns. We'll certainly be getting action up here when a battalion of infantry is supported by two battalions of artillery. That will be the setup beginning with tomorrow. That's eight times the normal amount."

Each time the engineers were ready to set off a charge, they notified me in time to set two cameras, one for Corporal Padgitt to operate and one for me, so we could catch the blast from different angles. Then the men set charges in a "beehive"—a device used to give downward force to the explosion—and shouted a warning for everyone to get out of the range of flying rocks. A great black cloud rose up with a roar, and after the hail of rocks subsided, they wired TNT blocks, and off went another great black burst. At intervals, an angle dozer pushed the rubble aside; it would be used later as gravel, for gravel, I was informed, is a precious commodity in war.

"After the armistice they ought to carve the bulldozer in marble," said Lieutenant Colonel Dziuban. "If they're making statues of heroes, it's been a hero all right."

We were having mess of K rations under a camouflaged tent half when we heard an air burst coming into the gorge behind us. An air burst is an antipersonnel shell, set to explode not on impact but a certain distance above the ground, possibly twenty or fifty feet, to wound or kill whatever men may be below. In ravines like those we were in, it has a second objective. It acts as a placer shell, for since its burst is visible to the enemy observers, their aim can be adjusted on targets too deep in the cliffs for observation of a direct hit.

"They're after that new Bailey bridge," said the Colonel. The long bridge we had crossed shortly before we reached the road block was in a gorge deep enough so that the Germans, even from the tops of their mountain peaks, couldn't see it. But they could aim an air burst above it—which they could see—work out their mathematical corrections, and adjust their fire accordingly.

I knew that this was a strategic bridge because it was carrying a constant flow of supplies for the same push which the new plateauful of artillery was intended to support.

When we heard the next air burst sail in, Colonel Dziuban jumped up. "I'm going down there to see what's going on," he said. "You can come along if you want to."

I didn't have to ask Padgitt if he wanted to come. He had loaded the cameras and himself into the back of the jeep in a single motion, and we took off around the bend.

We rounded the base of the mountain, circled the ruins of the power plant, and then were out in the open part of the gorge facing the new bridge. A wisp of greasy black smoke was rising over the road in front of us.

I noticed something strange about the road. This was the first time I was to see it, but I was to meet it many times again. In a peculiar way the road had suddenly gone dead. Where just before you would have seen soldiers all over the place, engineers working, people cleaning out the ditches, men driving trucks and jeeps, suddenly the road has become perfectly quiet.

This is what happens to a road during a shelling. I think if you had your eyes closed you would smell it. It wasn't that there were not people there. There were many people—soldiers lining the ditches and crouched behind big rocks, some lying flat behind the ruined fragments of an old stone wall. They looked up at us curiously as we drove past. Several deserted trucks were in the road. I remember a motorcycle turned over on its side with the engine still running, and I recall seeing a jeep—or rather it was part of a jeep; the rear wheels were there but the front was missing.

Just then another shell sailed in and made a direct hit on a "protective truck" which was mounted with a .50-caliber machine gun and had been drawn up near the new bridge to defend the men working there against strafing planes. The truck burst into flames, its gas tanks caught fire, and the ammunition it carried for its ack-ack gun began exploding in all directions. As Colonel Dziuban stopped the jeep, giving me a chance to take pictures of it, a tall column of dirty yellow-orange smoke began rising up and curling over the Volturno River valley.

The Germans were very kind to me that day, because they gave me just time to take the two pictures I wanted before we heard another scream overhead, and made for the nearest ditch. It was a muddy ditch, but suitable for our purpose, as it had a high mudbank in back of us, which gave a certain amount of protection, and it afforded a clear view of the bridge the Germans were trying to hit. The shells were landing on the road opposite us, directly across the narrow bend of the Volturno, and Padgitt kept handing me film packs and reloading cameras as fast as I could shoot with them.

In a curious succession we could hear the sounds of the shelling. First would be the screaming whistle overhead, then a lapse of time which seemed like minutes but could only have been a split second, and we would see the shell bursting on the road opposite us. Then after a lapse of time—because light travels faster than sound—which again seemed like minutes but must have been less than a second, the roar of the exploding shell would come back to us.

Immediately we would hear another whistle, this time a little higher-pitched or lower-pitched than the one before—you can't help wondering whether the changed pitch means it is coming closer or farther away—then we would see the burst and hear the explosion.

Colonel Dziuban had it worked out to a science. We would hear the scream, and he would say, "You can stand up now for a second," I would pop up and take my picture, and then we would duck before the next shell came.

Finally there was a letup. "That was thirty-two rounds in eight minutes," said Corporal Padgitt, and we made for the jeep.

"I guess we can consider the subject covered," I remarked, thinking that if the Corporal could sound so matter-of-fact, I would try to sound nonchalant, too.

We had just started climbing into the jeep when we heard another whooshing sound overhead, and we hurried back to our ditch. The shells were falling closer to the bridge now, and, incidentally, closer to us.

Then one shell hit the bridge but only struck a corner of the abutment, knocking off a bit of masonry. I don't know whether Corporal Padgitt was still counting rounds at this point. But I do know he was handing me equipment as I needed it with all the *savoir-faire* of a portrait assistant in a Fifth Avenue studio.

The Germans had bracketed their target now, and they switched from smoke shells to HE. The high explosives sent dull coils of black smoke rising from each hit; it was a very unphotogenic type of shell.

At last a shell fell directly under the bridge, where it could have done a great deal of damage. It made a great splash of water, but that shell was a dud. It would have cost us the whole central span if it hadn't been.

At this point a Piper Cub flew overhead and hedgehopped its way toward the enemy. I could see why foot soldiers have such affection for these Grasshoppers. The Cub seemed like a brave little friend up there, and it turned out later that it was.

"This is a good time to go forward," said Colonel Dziuban. "The Germans will probably hold fire for a little while; they won't want that Cub to spot their gun positions."

We jumped into our jeep and drove away from the river crossing, and had reached the base of the mountain when the shelling started again. Looking back, we saw that the Germans had shortened their gun range just enough so that the shells were falling in the road right where we had been sitting. I always felt that that Piper Cub had saved my life.

All the rest of the afternoon I photographed where the engineers were removing the boulder from the road. While the men blasted away we could still hear the shells coming in and dropping behind us—we were more or less protected behind the mountain. The Germans were evidently determined to knock out that new bridge. The rocky walls of the ravine picked up the echoes in a horrible way. Every time a shell came in, it sounded like a baby wailing through the gorge.

I kept thinking, "Well, of course, we're going to have to go back over that bridge in order to get home." It became a sort of obsession with me, but I decided I might as well go on taking pictures. However, I couldn't keep the idea from turning over in my mind. I thought there must be some other way to go home, but I knew there wasn't. In about an hour we would start traveling along that same road where we had been pinned to the ditch; we would go over the bridge where the Germans were aiming, along the stretch of road where we had watched the shells falling. For one brief minute we would drive behind a hill where we would have protection from direct enemy observation, and then we would have a long stretch of road, above which the enemy sat in his OP and looked down at us.

At last it was almost dusk and time to go home. It is important for all extra traffic to get off the roads before nightfall, to leave the highways clear for the heavy convoys bringing up supplies to the front. A very businesslike, gray-haired engineer came to call for us, according to our prearranged plan. He was the Commanding Officer of the Engineering Corps, Colonel Dziuban's immediate superior, and was to be my host during my stay with the engineers. Even then, preoccupied as I was, I noticed how the expression on his face amusingly matched the expression of the eagles on his shoulders.

We piled into the Colonel's command car, Corporal Padgitt with the driver in front, the Colonel, Captain Deutschle, and I in back. "Don't fasten that door too tight," the Colonel directed, and we started toward the opening in the gorge.

As we rounded the mountain and again came out on open road, once more we saw a little greasy smoke escaping into the air just in front of us. Once more the road had that lifeless look. As many soldiers were there, but they were somewhat rearranged by that time. I suppose they had been in and out of their ditches a dozen times that afternoon, trying to get their work done in between.

The driver pulled the command car to a full stop before turning into the bridge. The Colonel turned to the Captain and said, "All right with you, Captain?"

The Captain answered, "It's up to you, Colonel."

"No, I want to consult you first," said the Colonel. "How do you feel about it?"

"Colonel, it's up to you," the Captain replied.

Nobody asked me how I felt about it.

The Colonel said, "Well, if it's got your number on it, it's got your number on it. Let's go ahead." And ahead we went.

We were just turning into the bridge when I heard a whistle. It was a long whistle, and I thought it would never stop. Suddenly I realized it was our driver whistling to keep his courage up.

On the far side of the bridge stood a white-faced MP; his essential job was to keep traffic spaced widely as it crossed the bridge. "That's a mean post he's had today," said the Colonel to us, and leaning out he shouted, "Good boy. You're doing a fine job."

Once over the bridge we swung into the part of road on which I had watched the shells falling; then for one blessed moment we were hidden from enemy view behind the hill—and again were out in the open, traveling over the long stretch where the Germans had direct observation.

We were about to cross the Hot-Spot Bridge when we ran into a traffic jam—a very bad thing in wartime. The MP's who do our police duty are very efficient and usually are able to prevent road congestion. But the Hot-Spot Bridge had become a bottleneck, and there was nothing to do but sit and wait.

While we were waiting, an air burst sailed in ahead of us. We couldn't see whether or not any damage had been done. Then at last the traffic started and rolled on slowly but steadily, and we were swept on with it.

We crossed the Hot-Spot Bridge, and on the other side I saw two boys lying there so quietly they looked as though they were asleep. One was on one side of the road and one on the other. There hadn't been time to move them, and the traffic flowed on in a slow, steady stream between them. These soldiers lay there quite peacefully, and in such natural positions it seemed almost as though they must be resting by the roadside. As we drove on I glanced back and saw that one boy had lost half his head and the other had lost all of his face.

It was dark when we reached the Engineers' Command Post. The colonel went to the phone at once; he was in constant contact with all parts of the front where his men were working.

From the reports we found out that just after we had left the area the Germans had hit our Bailey bridge, but only managed to land a shell on one corner of it. Two panels were knocked off, but within eight minutes the engineers had patched it together and traffic was flowing on again.

CHAPTER 6

Monks and Engineers

MY LIFE while working with the engineers more nearly approached a routine existence than any other I lived while covering the war. This was largely because I had regular quarters instead of living like a gypsy with my bedroll in foxholes and dugouts. By contrast, my billet seemed quite normal. I lived in a monastery with fifty monks and I slept in a cell.

This was a happy solution to what had at first seemed a bit of a problem. When I arrived, the hospitable engineers were eager to make me as comfortable as possible, but there was no room to give me private accommodations in the cluster of tents where they had their quarters. Within walking distance, however, was a fourteenth-century monastery. The engineers, having struck up something of a friendship with the monks, prevailed upon their Father Superior to put me up.

My cell opened out on an echoing, vaulted corridor, lining which were scores of identical cells inhabited by the holy fathers. Often at night I could hear them pattering back and forth to visit each other, chattering loudly among themselves, and unexpectedly breaking into gales of laughter like youngsters in boarding school.

The plumpest monk was Fra Mario: to the engineers he was "Friar Tuck." The smallest monk was Fra Antonio, called "The KP." Friar Tuck's amazing girth was so disproportionate to his height that the neighboring engineers, who should know about matters like pedal locomotion, never figured out how his legs under his black frock managed to carry him so easily about the corridors. The KP was a surprise to all of us, because although we had not given the matter much previous thought, we had never realized that monks could come so small.

The KP was so named because he spent hours tagging about the skirts of Friar Tuck in the stone-paved kitchen. There in the midst of whirling steam, looking like a fattened-up witch over his caldrons, the friar sometimes turned out miraculous concoctions for his friends, the *Americanos*. His most frequent dish was something resembling Southern spoonbread, which appeared with countless varieties of trimming and sauces and was known as *pasta*. Even more popular than *pasta* was Friar Tuck's spinach. It was hard to tell whether there was more spinach or more garlic in the big wooden bowls that emerged from the kitchen.

The hours which Friar Tuck spent away from his bowls and kettles were largely taken up with his embroidery. He had a flair for roses. I believe that only on the floor of heaven, into which undoubtedly the good father had been granted special insight, could roses like his grow. Certainly no earthly blooms ever possessed such an intricacy of un-folding petals, such a blinding brilliance of vermilion and scarlet.

But the obliging friar was always ready to lay these fascinating em-broideries aside for more drab needlework. Every time one of the *Americanos* came over with a shirt or a field jacket that needed mending, Friar Tuck set to work. He had a sewing machine in his cell. He was very good with patches and reinforcements, and he was outstanding with insignia, which he appliquéd in place by means of a double cross-stitch.

Since the monastery had been continuously inhabited by the same re-ligious order since the fourteenth century, I suppose the monks had grown accustomed, in their worshipful way, to the presence of the relic of a saint which reclined full length in a deep stone niche behind Gothic pointed doors at the foot of the main staircase. But our engineers—and there were a number who liked to come over and visit—never got used to being on visiting terms with a mummy. They were inordinately im-pressed with it, and I think the monks were rather pleased at the way the engineers peeped between the pointed doors whenever they came over, as if they wanted to see how the mummy was getting along.

The central courtyard of the monastery was a pleasant place in the mornings. The sun (when it shone—which was by no means always in "sunny Italy") marked the hour on an ancient sundial and cast endless arched shadows from the colonnaded porch which surrounded the court in a perfect square.

Often a handful of engineers came down to get hot water to shave. I would see them with their helmets full of soapy water propped up on the balustrade. The friars filed by, filling their pails and kettles from the central well. "*Buon giorno!*" each friar would say. "*Buon giorno!*" each lather-covered engineer would reply. Tiny Fra Antonio, the KP, always lingered in the kitchen doorway, unable to take his eyes off the *Americanos* while they scrubbed and shaved.

My early-morning ablutions were conducted not in the courtyard, but in a large stone cell, down the hall from my tiny one, which the monks had fitted with certain primitive attempts at plumbing. The Commanding Officer of the Engineering Corps, the Colonel who had picked us up in the gorge, came over early each morning to help me plan my day and made a practice of knocking at my door to awaken me. Then he would precede me into this dark cavern with its plumbing, make a preliminary investigation, and emerge with the words, "Coast's all clear." While I scrubbed, the CO stood guard outside the door to make sure I was not interrupted by monks, who might also wish to use their plumbing facilities.

The Colonel in command was one of those dignified, martial personages, with iron-gray hair, a clipped mustache, and an inflexible insistence on discipline, the type that even a layman instantly recognizes as "old Army." For reasons of censorship I may not mention him by name, but since a day came when he remarked, "Call me Tommy," we shall call him Tommy.

Tommy followed a regular routine of leaving me at the Senior Officers' Mess tent while he climbed the slippery hill through the olive grove for his morning conference with a still more exalted individual, the brigadier general in command of the corps. The general lived in a trailer which was reached by teetering over scattered boards loosely laid in a sea of mud.

There was nothing remarkable about the Senior Officers' Mess tent where I was deposited for breakfast, except the table top, which someone had rescued almost intact from the ruins of a demolished village. It was a thick slab of Carrara marble as white as the counter of a soda fountain. Once I had been invited to dinner at the general's mess. There was nothing remarkable about his mess tent either, except the tablecloth, a large one of fine linen left behind by some Italian general retreating with the German army.

Tommy returned from the corps officers' conference at about the time I finished my coffee and powdered eggs, which had been quite palatably scrambled by a most competent mess sergeant. (In the Army you rate the mess sergeant according to how well he disguises the powdered eggs or Spam he feeds you.)

Both the Colonel and I would take some of the lifesavers and hard candies which always stood in a bowl in the middle of the table, and put them into our pockets, not only for ourselves, but as handouts to the Italian children who were always crying for *caramelle*. Then we walked up the road to the Corps Command Post, which was on the second floor of a cracked plaster farmhouse in a room with leaded casement windows hung with flypaper. The walls were covered with maps and charts. A small area in the center of the room was raised to volcanic heat by a tiny brazier, a prized item which somebody had picked up. One yard away from the coals everybody shivered.

The Colonel took his field telephone off its hook on the wall and began checking his many forward installations. During these conversations Tommy, nursing his various bridges which were growing along the front, always reminded me of a gardener watching his flowers bloom. He inquired about rainfall, flood conditions, and the previous night's shell damage. Then he consulted a miraculous set of aerial photographs through a stereoscope. The pictures were pieced together, mosaic fashion, over a sheet of illuminated glass in such a way that when you looked through the stereoscope the peaks and rims of the gorges jumped at you, and the demolition which had to be repaired fell into three-dimensional perspective. Through this device, the engineers estimated the width and depth of the gorges to be bridged, and calculated the type and amount of materials needed.

Weaving his eyes over this luminous sheet of glass, like a crystal-gazer, Colonel Tommy could plot the enemy's destruction in advance. In the twelve-mile stretch of Colli-Atina road, the Colonel knew that thirty-eight acts of demolition would occur by the time the Germans were pushed completely out of this area. In the case of those most imminent, he already had the bridge parts loaded up on trucks, ready to rush to the front the instant they were needed, so that our infantry could press ahead with almost no loss of time.

The Colonel picked several installations to inspect and arranged for me to go along to take pictures. When the locations for the day's work had been selected, we piled into the Colonel's command car, Corporal Padgitt in front with the driver, Colonel Tommy and I in the rear. Later on we made other trips and often one of the captains came along. Usually it was good-natured Captain Joe Deutschle, with whom I worked a great deal. Sometimes it would be Captain Harry Morris, whose experience in civilian life as an architect of low-cost modern housing projects in Detroit made him a competent officer with the engineers. I was always amused at the way the youthful but scholarly face of Captain Morris, with his silver-rimmed spectacles, nearly disappeared from sight when he put on his helmet.

This trip was typical, however; we settled into the back seat of the command car with our knees up to our chins, because the floor had been piled deep with sandbags to break the force of the explosion in case we ran over a mine.

Once we had swung out into the open and started down into the Volturno valley, the benign atmosphere of my monastery fell away like a dream.

"This valley has always been bad news," said Tommy.

Along the tops of the ridges above Venafro, we could see sporadic white smoke bursts where our shells were striking at enemy gun positions. Every so often, black puffs mottled the sky from ack-ack guns shooting toward enemy reconnaissance planes too high for us to see. Once a brief dogfight took place over our heads, and we leaned out to watch, following the course of the fight, as though in skywriting, until the thready vapor trails of the planes disappeared over the mountain.

As we drove along I was fascinated by the road signs. At every turn and crossroad clusters of them pointed to ordnance repair depots, water points, field hospitals, and ammo dumps. The installation of these signs is included in the multiple functions of the engineers. Near a one-way bridge a new sign was being put up for the French troops, PONT À SENS UNIQUE. Just beyond a water point another sign, POINT D'EAU was being installed. "For the Goums," said Colonel Tommy. The most frequent signs had to do with dispersal of traffic. A traffic jam can be murder near the front if the congested stretch of road gets a plastering from shells, or a burst of machine-gun bullets from a strafing plane. Every short distance there was a warning sign, 50-YARD INTERVAL, which if kept usually guarantees that a strafer will not get more than one vehicle per attack.

Evidently some of the Engineering Corps sign painters got tired of the similarity of wording, for we began passing rhymed series, strung out "Burma Shave" fashion along the highway. One such sequence of five signs, decorated with drawings of a bespectacled soldier being dive-bombed by a frightening plane with swastikas, read:

there was a gi near venafro
who couldn't read signs by golly
jerry planes were overhead
and now he is dead
so solly my boy so solly

Tommy was somewhat irritated that members of his Engineering Corps were wasting paint, but finally as we kept passing more jingles he was moved to little rhymed recollections of his own. "Have you heard this one?" he asked, and recited:

Lives of engineers remind us
We could write our names in blood;
And departing leave behind us
Half our faces in the mud.

This poetic interval was brought to a halt by our running into a real traffic jam. "That's a fine way to get bombed and shelled," said the Colonel, "with everybody getting all jammed up bumper to bumper," and leaping out he started directing traffic himself.

"Spread out!" he shouted. "You're fine targets for Jerry; all lined up like turkeys in a ditch." He began ordering the traffic about with such terrifying authority that I suspected that when he was a little boy he had wanted to be a traffic cop. We could hear him talking savagely in a monotone to himself. "Let a few of them get scattered around so they can't get up again, and they'll learn."

"That's telling 'em," said Padgitt from the front seat, and then started shaking with stifled laughter at the faces of a few incautious jeep drivers who were trying to sneak ahead of the line and were startled out of their wits to see the Old Man himself directing traffic.

"Enough of those Jerries killing us without our trying to kill ourselves," roared the Colonel, sending the offenders back to the very end of the line.

Finally the traffic began slowly to roll on again; we went with it, and Tommy hopped back into the command car in such a cheerful mood that I suspected I was right and he enjoyed these chances to play policeman.

As we came out into the flood plain of the Volturno, I caught my first glimpse of the "Delirium Tremens Bridge."

"That's a beautiful bridge," I exclaimed.

"That's what Jerry thinks," said the Colonel. "Jerry keeps going after that bridge like a duck after a June bug."

Jerry had indeed, we found, been after the bridge that very morning. There had been a dive-bombing attack, but a patrol of Spitfires had driven off the raiders. Just before daylight there had been an attempt at sabotage. Four Germans loaded with dynamite had slipped through the lines at midnight, wearing their summer uniforms which are so similar in color to those of our paratroopers that they had almost reached the bridge undetected. Only when some Italians asked them for cigarettes was their insignia noticed, and they were turned over to some American Negro troops for arrest. Since the saboteurs came in uniform they would be, according to international law, held as prisoners of war, not shot as spies. But the engineering bridge gang, who were discussing the incident excitedly, felt that the spy line was dangerously close.

This double-triple Bailey, the "DT" as it was called, had had a strenuous war history. Three times it had been rebuilt. Twice the floating pontoon crossings, which had preceded the present structure, had been swept away by floods. Then the engineers put in a double-single Bailey (double span wide; single span high). This, too, began washing away when wreckage accumulating against the remains of the old Italian piers began forming a dam. Overnight the fierce, pent-up stream began forcing its way out, cutting into the banks like a spade, and actually changing the course of the river.

Engineers working up to their waists in water and paddling around in rubber boats rescued the sections of the double-single Bailey, and began reinforcing it into a double-double. When I arrived with the Colonel, the engineers were adding still a third tier for strength, converting the double-double into a double-triple, or "DT." Small wonder that it was nicknamed "Delirium Tremens."

Much of the incredible speed with which the engineers rebuild demolished bridges and span shell gaps in roads is due to the portable design of the Bailey, the most remarkable bridge in the history of military operations. It can cross any gap up to 240 feet without pontoons, and with pontoons the stretch is almost limitless.

The bridge parts are interchangeable and light, the heaviest requiring only six men to lift it. The prefabricated sections are ten feet long, and only one steel pin is needed for each joint. The Bailey fits together like a gigantic Meccano toy and, after being built on rollers on the edge of a river, can be pushed over by the building crew without mechanical aid.

Time schedule is everything in building bridges in a war area. While the double-triple over the Volturno was under construction, traffic was being carried temporarily over a floating trestle treadway that had been thrown across upstream. The new Bailey had to be finished in time to carry the heavy convoys that would start at dusk for the front.

"What's the time schedule?" Colonel Tommy inquired of the officer in charge.

"I'm phoning Traffic Control that we can take an uninterrupted load at four."

"Now you're cooking with gas," Tommy approved. "You sure of your load capacity?"

"The only thing is headroom, Colonel." And while the two officers discussed the requirements of a "class forty load," I began photographing the intricate latticed panels swarming with men. They were pinning together lateral stays and cribbing with such astonishing speed that I could watch the bridge growing before my eyes.

Under the center of the new span, but not touching it, was a broken masonry arch, the last remnant of the Italian bridge which had been blown up by the Germans. As it was clogging the stream it had to be blasted away.

The charges were placed by men in rubber boats, and when everything was ready for setting off the TNT, the men scrambled down off the bridge to be out of the way of flying rocks. There were two points of view I wanted, so I posted Padgitt at one of them, with the Rolleiflex, and occupied the other myself with a Linhof. Colonel Tommy called warning signals so we could both be ready to catch the blast. Then the Colonel gave the word to blow, and a ravishingly beautiful geyser rose high in the air and descended lazily in a shower of diamonds. I had time to snatch two separate pictures; the corporal had been quick enough to catch three.

"Jiminy, if *Life* should print one of my pictures instead of yours!" the Corporal exclaimed. "Just only one shot! Boy, won't you get the razz!"

Well, the censor had the last laugh on that one. The Corporal did get the best picture. Exposure right; filter right; focus perfect; composition marvelous. It was a honey! It was so good that it revealed the construction of the bridge, and was censored out.*

After the explosion, the bridge gang scrambled back with their tools like monkeys up a trellis and several GI's took off in the rubber boats that are always around a bridge job. They were after the fish which floated to the top, stunned by the blast, and they paddled about until they had scooped up several helmetfuls.

It was 11:30 and mess lines had begun forming. We lined up at the rear end of the mess truck for hot C rations with canned peas and meatballs, which were all poured together with fruit-salad mixture into our mess kits. We were just making our way through the mud to sit down on a log when I found myself suddenly grabbed from behind and whirled off my feet. I was amazed when I realized it was the Colonel. Despite the fact that we were Tommy and Peggy to each other, he had until now been consistently formal in his behavior. "What's all this?" I gasped; but instead of answering he threw me down in a crevasse between two rock piles and crawled in beside me.

Then I knew what it was—a strafer. A rising, crunching sound was coming up the road. From under the rim of my helmet I could see the engineering gang who had been clinging all over the spans of the Bailey, working their way down like circus performers.

That's a rough place to be just now, I thought.

"Keep your head down," Tommy said.

As I ducked, I caught out of the corner of my eye a glimpse of the strafer with its painted swastika. Behind it were two more planes, a pair of Spitfires hot on its tail.

It was only another second before people were pulling themselves to their feet again. The Spits had chased the ME off, and we could watch all three racing away over the ridge above Venafro until the mountains blocked them from sight.

The relief was so great we were hilarious. The boys pulled my mess kit out of the mud. "Anyway, it's good eating mud," they said, and brought me another dose of C rations. "We engineers get so we can't enjoy a meal without eating some mud with it."

We were all excited by the close shave of the bulldozer operator, who

* As this book was going to press, Padgitt's picture was released. You will find it with the other Bailey Bridge photographs.

came up during lunch to show us his helmet. He had been at the wheel of the dozer when the ME started up the road. Any vehicle is a bad place during a strafing, and he had streaked across the road in time to jump behind a low wall. He was just crouching down when he was thrown over on his back so violently that he thought for a minute his neck had been broken. When he pulled himself together he found that he was quite unhurt, but that a hit had creased his helmet down the middle like a Homburg.

So, while we finished our C rations and drank our canteen cups of cocoa, everybody began matching narrow escapes. The best story came from a second lieutenant who had gotten up during the night, and stepped out of his tent for the usual purpose, during which time a brief strafing of the tent area took place. After it was over, everybody visited around and made sure that no one had been hurt. When the excitement died down, the lieutenant crawled back into bed and was annoyed to find his cot wet. Evidently someone had dropped his canteen there with the cover unscrewed, he thought. In the morning he found that his canteen had a hole in it and a 20-mm. shell had passed through his mattress where his chest would have been and had buried itself unexploded under his cot.

CHAPTER 7

Foxhole Studio

I HAVE ALWAYS been sorry I never got to know that Signal Corps photographer better. We shared the same ditch when we got caught between the two contestants during an artillery duel. As I learned later, he was a most interesting person.

It was hard to tell whose shells were passing closer to the tops of our heads, theirs or ours. Ours whooshed over with a sound we found comforting, as though someone were stroking a bolt of raw silk. Theirs came on like quick blasts on a police whistle. "Close enough to part your hair down the middle," said Corporal Padgitt. The effect was not comforting.

The Corporal was at my side handing me film packs as I needed them. There was nothing much to photograph—just those monotonous fountains of earth and rock rising across the road and coming a little closer each time, as the Germans tried to "bracket" the target. But I have discovered that it contributes to a healthier state of mind to keep on working at such a time. Nothing else you can do, anyway; you're pinned to your ditch.

The Signal Corps photographer evidently felt the same way. Things had been happening so fast that I had not even seen him join us until I tried to edge upditch a little, where there was a better viewpoint, equally well protected. I had half pushed my way in front of someone when I realized that he had a movie camera in his hands and was using it very busily to record the barrage; it seemed a great coincidence to find another photographer in the same ditch. I am not especially noted for politeness when getting pictures, and I doubt if anyone's manners are at their best during a shelling. However, there is a certain code of behavior, and even then my professional habits asserted themselves; I could not push another photographer out of the way.

We never had time to speak to each other. The exchange of shells ended as quickly as it had begun, the engineering gang swarmed out of

59

the holes and gullies where they had thrown themselves, and the Signal Corps photographer somehow disappeared in the shuffle. Later I learned that he was Technical Sergeant Peter Ratoff, brother of Gregory Ratoff, the Hollywood director. And still later I learned about his final act of courage.

About two weeks later, and not far from the place where we had met, Sergeant Ratoff was working at a Chemical CP. This Command Post was located in one of those small pink plaster farmhouses which dot the Italian countryside. The Chemical Section, which comes under the engineers, has charge of throwing smoke screens and laying smoke pots for camouflage.

We know that Sergeant Ratoff tried to photograph that JU when it swooped out of the sky. We know, because of his camera. It wasn't the safest thing to do, but there is no safety, anyway, at such a time, and those fine action pictures always represent a narrow escape on the part of the photographer. Suddenly the dive-bomber headed right for the CP. In less than a minute it was over. The building had been wrecked; the colonel in command and his staff had been instantly killed, and not a trace was ever found of the sergeant again. But his movie camera was still turning freakishly, quite undamaged; a tribute to a brave man who died at his job. He was reported "missing in action" by the War Department.

On the day I encountered Sergeant Ratoff, Padgitt and I were visiting different types of bridges: the primitive bypass type, thrown hastily across streams and gullies for an infantry advance; the sturdier trestle crossing which is built as soon as the engineers can install a heavier job. These are replaced by Baileys as soon as it is not too hot to risk the materials.

There was a good deal of bridge building and road clearance going on that day, for the Goums were coming. For miles back the roads were lined with these French native troops. They sat by the roadside, waiting for darkness, the reddish-brown stripes of the burnooses they wore blending with the landscape. These Goums were seasoned troops, veterans of the North African and Sicilian campaigns. They looked sturdy and somewhat frightening, with their fierce knives in their belts. In addition to their primitive weapons, they carried our new Lend-Lease M-1 rifles.

Everyone hoped the Goums would do well. They were replacing a division of our American boys who had been in the lines for sixty-nine days and badly needed a rest. Truckfuls of weary, bearded soldiers were being brought to the rear that day. They would be taken to the fine delousing plant just out of shell range. This had been newly set up with shower baths and tentfuls of quartermaster supplies where the boys could exchange their filthy clothes for new boots and field jackets. After delousing, they would be sent all clean and shaven to Naples or Sorrento for a short leave. After that, although we did not know it at the time, they would take part in the amphibious action of which we had already heard rumors, and which later materialized at Anzio.

Colonel Tommy was busy helping to get the French engineers and artillery sections installed. He had left us at one of his bridge projects, just before the artillery duel took place, and after it was over, the Corporal and I had tried to take a few pictures in the fading light. It was one of those cold, drizzling days so characteristic of winter in Italy. The bridge-building scene was as photogenic as gray blotting paper, a disadvantage we tried to overcome by the liberal use of peanut flash bulbs. The Corporal waded around in the shallow stream, stringing extension wires from my camera, which I tried to operate from a very wobbly rock.

Nobody minded the rain except Padgitt and me. Cloudy days are a protection against dive-bombers and strafers, and while they are no insurance against shelling, everybody was in a cheerful mood at the cessation of the barrage. It seemed a miracle that no shells had hit either the men or the bridge. In fact, there was a good deal of delighted comment on how many shells the Krauts could toss away without hitting anything. Also there had been a rather high percentage of duds. That always made everybody feel good. We never knew whether the duds were caused by hasty and faulty manufacture or by deliberate sabotage, but we always hoped it was the latter.

It was almost dusk when the Colonel came back to pick up Padgitt and me—and then all of us found to our horror that one of those enemy shells had not missed its mark. It had made a direct hit on a gun position just up the hill in back of us and killed the whole crew. "You could have carted the remains of that gun section away in a jeep," reported the Colonel.

To go home we had to pass through the same old bottleneck, over the Hot-Spot Bridge. This was a critical point. One of the most disturbing things about traveling to and from the front was the fact that there were only two main highways. Over both of them the enemy hung in his observation points, watching the traffic on the road below. Of the two main drags, the one we were on wound through Colli Pass; the other was the famous Highway Six, which supplied troops in the region of Cassino. As we started homeward, convoys of trucks were passing us with their loads of ammo and food for the front lines; but this evening we negotiated our journey through the tortuous pass without incident. Soon we were out in the clear and well on our way home.

I find it difficult to express the blessed relief, the quickening joy, with which you find yourself heading home from the front. Each mile in the road brings a lightening of the heart. Every day I had felt this surge of relief when I started homeward, and I was not proud of it.

What was happening to me, I wondered. For the last several years, as a war correspondent, I had been through my quota of bombings. I had been bombed in Barcelona, in Chungking, in Great Britain, North Africa, and Moscow. And, while nobody likes having bombs come too close, on the whole I had not minded it too much. You are a small target in a big place, and the chances are that you will pull through. You are willing to take your gambling chance in a city.

But shelling was different. Shelling was like a dentist with a drill. And with me, those shells had found the nerve.

Partly I think it was knowing how much science went into the aiming of those guns that made it so hard to take. The enemy was after a specific target. If you were unlucky enough to be at that target, from your point of view he was after you. It was intensely and horribly personal.

And another element came in. In many forms of danger you can do something about it, and that is your salvation. Even when we were chased in the cub by the four FW's, I was saved from fear by the fact that Captain Marinelli was doing something about it—and doing it so capably and swiftly that my confidence in him was instinctive and absolute. Also it happened so quickly that I hardly had time to think.

But with shelling, you simply can't do anything about it. You are pinned to your ditch, if you are lucky enough to get to a ditch, like a fox in a trap. You are at the will of the enemy. As a result, it is demoralizing.

As we drove homeward, I did a lot of wondering about how those boys felt who had to stay up there week after week, and sometimes month after month, without even the break of getting out of it for a night. Later I was to see the deathly strain on their faces, the growing numbness that enveloped them like a shroud. This numbness was their only defense against an anxiety that had become intolerable. To live in a state of mental paralysis was the only way they could stand it.

Even on that evening, which was early in my experience at the Fifth Army front, I felt somewhat guilty about being in as free a position as I was: to be able to go back even if only for a few hours and drink up that blessedness of being out of range. Later I came almost to regret my voluntary position. My decisions to go to the front depended on no one but myself and my desire to do a thorough and honest job. I used to wonder whether, if I were under orders, it wouldn't be easier.

I remember how one of the correspondents, an exceedingly brave and able man who has reported more wars than most of us will ever see, developed a peculiar apprehension just before he was due to return to America. He had previously charged ahead with the infantry every time a town was captured, and had exposed himself repeatedly to danger in his job of reporting from the front lines. Yet during his final ten days with the Fifth Army he made no trips to the front. He was sure that on his last trip he would get it.

I think it was that day at the trestle bridge when the shells had missed us, only to hit the gun crew who were answering the enemy, that I graduated. The school of thought I graduated from had been a soothing one as long as it lasted; I had had an irrational conviction that "nothing could ever happen to me." From then on, however, I never found myself in a foxhole without wondering whether I had tried my luck one too many times. After all, there is something to the law of averages.

The highway was thundering with convoys as we drove homeward, passing us as they carried their vital supplies to the front. Many of these trucks were driven by Negroes. The roads would be perfect hell as they got farther forward, where the danger from traffic accidents without lights was even greater than the menace of enemy artillery.

We grew drowsy. We napped a little, and when we woke up we sang a little: old standbys like *Carry Me Back to Old Virginny*, to which Tommy added a splendid tenor; *Juanita*, to which he sung a beautiful alto, and finally *O Sole Mio*, on which Padgitt surprisingly joined in from the front seat.

As we drove homeward the fine rain died away and the moon came up over the dark hills. We knew we would be late for mess, so we fished around in our pockets for those hard suckers supplied with our rations, candies which come in so handy at such times. Out of an unappetizing tangle of grubby notes, pencil stubs, and camera odds and ends, which I carried in my field jacket, I produced a prize: a Tootsie Roll I had bought at the PX. I divided the sticky mass as evenly as possible among the Colonel, the Corporal, and the sergeant driver, and marveled at the things which take on value to adult men in war.

A red star rose over the mountain. It was an artillery wind guide, a lighted balloon sent up by the gun crews to compute deflection data. It hung like a kerosene lamp just above the horizon. The entire landscape was whitewashed by the moon.

"I've come to hate moonlight," commented Colonel Tommy, "ever since my best friend was killed on a moonlight night. Strafing pilots can see too much."

When we arrived at the CP, Tommy went up to his stereoscope and charts and I walked down the road to the monastery hoping that Friar Tuck would give me something to eat. I found that he was already giving the junior officers a feed in a great dungeonlike vault in the basement. From the walls a fresco of faded saints looked down on what must have been, in their centuries-long experience, a unique scene.

Friar Tuck sat on a chest in the middle of the room, surrounded by a group of officers shouting with laughter. They were teaching the friar to smoke his first cigar.

The inevitable bowl of garlic and spinach was there, and with it we had slabs of some wonderful honeydew melon someone had obtained in an obscure trade with the peasants. The native red wine which had been so plentiful when the Americans came in had grown hard to get. So we roared our welcome when "Suitcase Simpson" came into the dungeon, rolling a straw-covered bottle which must have held five gallons. "Drink up that vino," he said, "and you'll change your identity." "Suitcase Simpson" had earned his name because his feet were so big. Outside the junior officers' group he was known as Captain Robert Darling, Supply Officer.

We drank vino from our canteen cups, and ate dripping melon slices with the spinach, while Friar Tuck made faces over his cigar.

It was always interesting to me how consumption of food of any kind at any time would start a conversation about beefsteaks. There was no limit to the variations that a discussion of steaks could take; endless consideration went into that eagerly anticipated event in the dim future —the first steak order when you got back in the good old U. S. A.

"Just pass a match under mine and hand it to me," said Harry Morris.

"I'll take mine medium with French-fried onions," was "Suitcase Simpson's" vote.

"I'll have to put a piece of mud on the edge of the plate and eat it like mustard," said Joe Deutschle.

"I'm going to order a sirloin four inches thick, with a piece of Spam on the side, and I'll just put that Spam on the floor and say, 'To hell with you,'" said Major Arrasmith.

Four-inch steaks and eggs with shells on them had become symbols of home.

Major Bill Arrasmith had many observations on the egg situation. "Funny thing," he remarked. "In Africa we could buy quantities of eggs. In Italy we can't buy eggs but we can get all the chickens we want. How did all the eggs get over there and all the chickens here? Who separated them?"

Major William Strudwick Arrasmith was a great hearty fellow. In civilian life he had been an architect for most of the Greyhound Bus Stations throughout the country; now he served as Corps Planning Officer. "Arrow" came, he told me, from "the South, where men are men and women are oh, so happy about it."

It was a lot of fun to be with the engineers. They had great *esprit de corps* and worked together like brothers. The combat engineers enjoy enormous prestige in the Army; in the unwritten social ledger they are rated close to pilots as glamour boys. This prestige is a deserved tribute to their constant readiness to pave the way for infantry troops and artillery, no matter how hazardous the advance. Like all men in dangerous professions, they joked about it. During a break-through, they told me, "Jerry just sits up there and watches, and then aims at the one man who has a castle on his collar."

They had had their hands full during the recent floods, with banks and piers being washed away overnight, and the river changing its course every time the water rose. "We had a hard time," they said, "keeping the Volturno twisted around so it would go under our bridges."

"You know, those bridge parts by the time they get them shipped over here are worth more than their weight in gold," the engineers told me, "and they are very heavy."

And they let me in on their latest joke on themselves. It was about a span which hung in lonely grandeur across one of the wildest mountain gorges. No wheels would roll over it; no highway connected it with the world. It would hang there like a monument forever. When our troops made their first advance through these mountains, the engineers had thrown together a series of temporary bridges, which served to rush supplies over the gorges until a permanent road was opened. Then the front lines changed, and new bridges were needed in a hurry in forward areas, so they removed the chain, working from each end. When this job was done, they found one span left in the middle. It was impossible to move it; in fact, no one could reach it. "It's going to be there for a good long time," they chuckled, "so we named it The Engineers' Memorial Bridge."

It was bedtime, and the engineers went out to climb their muddy hill to their tents, and I went up to my cell. I had just arrived when there was a knock on the door. It was one of the draftsmen, an avid camera enthusiast, who volunteered each night for the kindest deed he could have done: he called for my boots and leggings, always unbelievably weighted down with mud, and had them washed and dried by morning.

Then Colonel Tommy knocked. He had come to perform his last item on the day's agenda: to escort me as usual to the cave of plumbing, make sure it was clear of monks, and mount guard outside the door till I emerged from the murky depths. Then he saw me to my cell, said good night, and went back up the hill.

It was only during my last day at that station that I learned the enlisted personnel had somehow found out all about the Colonel's little chaperoning trips and were taking a delighted interest in these unprecedented activities of their commanding officer. During this ritual, anyone who asked for the CO was given the gleeful reply: "The Colonel's doing latrine duty."

As I climbed into my narrow cot, the walls of my equally narrow cell reverberated to the confused voices of the guns outside. Always I have been an incurable reader in bed; even war could not break me of the habit. Obeying the blackout, I made a kind of tent of my blankets, and in approved boarding-school fashion read under the covers by flashlight. My book was an appropriate one. Someone had given me a weighty volume called *The Tools of War*, by James R. Newman, which dealt with the development of firearms, siegecraft, and fortifications from the beginning of recorded history. It traveled with me throughout the Italian campaign until it became as worn as an old coat.

So, hunched under the covers, I tried to catch up on some of those things which girls are not brought up to know about guns. I read up on range and elevation capacity, muzzle velocity, and recoil mechanisms of rifles and howitzers, of 105's and 155's, while those same 105's and 155's carried on their barking and stamping and roaring through the night.

When finally the text became unintelligible to me, I switched off my light and lay watching the square of window blaze up and fade with each clatter of guns. It was a good deal like trying to sleep over a noisy street crossing in the corner room of a cheap hotel. With the artillery flashing on and off like a neon sign outside my window, I had to put my head back under the covers again before I could drop off to sleep.

CHAPTER 8

The Muddy Road to Rome

"STRAIGHTENING UP this Italian situation is like trying to put tooth-paste back into tubes," said the ordnance officer as our jeep came to a full stop. We had struck a bottleneck before a floating pontoon bridge flung over the wide mainstream of the Volturno. On the marshy bank was a large group of Italian civilians who had been accumulating, wait-ing and hoping for a chance to get across. These were bombed-out fam-ilies who had fled to the hills with their scraps of bedding and furniture; now that their villages were in Allied hands they were seeking to return. Most of them, when they reached their destination, would find only piles of stones; those fortunate enough to have their houses still standing would find no wall without its shell scars, no roof without its gashes where flak fragments had plunged through.

As we sat there waiting our turn to cross, for the MP's were busy directing a large convoy over the floating trestle, keeping the trucks widely dispersed in case of a strafing, it occurred to me that there is no room for civilians in this war. Every town becomes a target and every road a strategic military thoroughfare. Citizens of a combat theater can-not stay at home without gambling with violent death; they cannot move without getting in the way of military supply lines.

The Germans have made efficient use of a new strategy of warfare, which employs living human bodies to clog the highways. Each military weapon has its answering measure; the countereffective is to keep refu-gees off the roads. So it becomes a common sight in Italy to see these miserable families on the march over footpaths in the hills and across the marshy fields. But when they reach the rivers they are checked. Since the Germans have destroyed all the bridges, and since those built by us represent a strategic link in the chain of supplies, the wretched congregation can do nothing but wait silently and patiently until the traffic control officers, who are naturally compassionate and will do the best they can, find enough of a letup in traffic to let them hurry across.

A lightening of traffic occurred once the convoy of trucks was safely over and the MP's held back the few scattered jeeps waiting and gave the civilians their chance to go across. Teetering precariously over the floating trestles they picked their way, carrying on their heads mattresses, chairs, bundles, and babies. At the end of the procession straggled those children too large to be carried, too small to keep up with the rest.

Next our jeep was allowed to cross. When we reached the opposite bank we were surrounded by children, chanting what has become almost the national song of Italy: *"Caramelle, caramelle."* We paused long enough to empty our pockets of the hard candies we always carried. An equitable distribution was impossible. It was painful to find ourselves the center of such a rush and scramble and laughter and tears, to have to hear the shouts of triumph and disappointed cries. I spotted one sad-faced mother at the side of the road, much too young for the two babies she carried, and I leaned out so she could safely reach the package of lifesavers I still had intact. The heavenly smile that lighted her thin face showed what a prize it was to her to get the entire package.

"I can't stand it when it's kids. God, it's awful," said the ordnance officer as we drove on. "I lie awake nights and suffer just thinking about them. And the darn little rascals can even grin at you."

Around the next bend in the road we met another sight I found interesting and moving in a totally different way. A gang of Negro soldiers were stacking ammo into those neat grocery-store piles which dot the roadsides near the front. In charge of them was a fine-looking officer. I noticed the bright eyes in the intelligent ebony-colored face even before I observed that he wore captain's insignia.

We stopped for a few minutes here while the officer accompanying me hopped out to do some checking on the arrival of the ordnance supplies. While I sat in the jeep waiting, I remembered some of the difficulties which, I had heard, confront Negroes who wish to increase their technical training while in the Army, and who seek to enter Officers' Candidate School. For this fellow to have risen to captain, I thought, he must be good.

The Negro troops who had been given the chance to work in forward areas, I reflected (and many of them had not been), had indeed earned their way. I had seen them doing Army service jobs all along the way from North Africa to Italy, stacking C rations, sorting worn clothes, working in road gangs, loading and unloading ships, and I had observed that they had done these jobs efficiently and well. Here, close to the battle zone, I had seen them transporting and handling ammunition stores along roads which represent selected German targets, where a shell hit on ammo costs the lives of all who handle it. I watched the colored captain moving briskly from group to group, directing the dispersal of the ammo load into widely separated piles, a precaution so that a direct shell hit will not blow up the whole countryside.

I had heard a good many discussions about whether Negroes could -stand up under shell fire. What makes anybody stand up under shell fire, I wondered. Part of it is knowing what you're fighting for (if you know); part of it is certainly *esprit de corps,* that instinct not to let the gang down. There had been little opportunity back in the States for Negroes and white men to develop mutually that spirit of not letting the gang down. Perhaps mutual trial by fire would bring about one constructive gain from this war. Already Negro pilots, flying with the 93rd Division in the Pacific and the 99th Pursuit Squadron in Italy, had made a potent contribution in this direction. Their records as fighters had earned the respect of Allied fliers everywhere.

As I watched the colored ammo squad, under the competent direction of their young commanding officer, I reflected that we owe these Negro soldiers a great deal. Although many of them at home have had advantages unequal to ours, still they are working side by side with their fellow Americans in the hope that in this war they are earning first-class citizenship.

My ordnance officer finished his check and climbed into the jeep. As we started on our way he turned to me and said something that made it hard to realize that this was the same man who had been so distressed half a mile back at the plight of the children. His remark was: "It makes my blood boil to see a nigger with bars on his shoulders."

We had been driving for about an hour when we passed a quartermaster bakery road sign. It was a wonderful break to arrive here just at noon. Anybody who has the slightest excuse will drop off at a field bakery for chow, because Army bakers have a reputation of serving a miraculous mess. Not only do they bake superior bread: their portable ovens are veritable Pandora's boxes, with unexpected delicacies popping out every time they open an oven door.

When our jeep stopped in the middle of the tent area, and we began climbing out with our cameras, we were instantly surrounded by a delighted crowd of bakery boys. "Why, it's *Life* come to take our pictures!" they exclaimed. Their happiness was unlimited that they should at last get some attention from the press. I had met this joyful reaction before among the laundry units, the delousing companies, the Quartermaster Corps, all those many behind-the-scene services which do their part so competently in the gigantic business of war. They are appreciated but seldom publicized.

Their CO came hurrying out to see what was going on.

"Why, it's my fellow Cornellian," exclaimed Captain Ernest on seeing me. Captain Herbert Ernest had been placed by the Army in the very job which he could do best. The son of a hotel man (his father is vice-president of the Commodore in New York), Herbert Ernest was a graduate of Cornell University's hotel-management course. The guest-is-always-right tradition undoubtedly ran in the Ernest family. With the Captain it was: the GI is always right. For the GI was indeed completely right about Army bread. All soldiers, except those too inaccessible to reach, get an average of half a pound of fresh bread a day. Despite the routine gripings about the monotony of C rations, which it is normal to hear even in our healthy, well-nourished Army, I have never heard anything but praise for our Army bread. If our own GI's rave about it, it is not surprising that German prisoners have been heard to exclaim, "The bread is so white it hurts your eyes."

As we sat down to mess, Captain Ernest had a freshly baked "sheet of bread," a tray of twelve loaves, brought to us, not only for us to eat, but so that he could deliver a thesis. The Captain set forth to analyze that bread in much the same terms I would use in describing a photographic negative. He discussed its quality, its density and texture, speed of processing, time and temperature treatment, its composition. When he finished his dissertation there was nothing left unsaid about bread; the only thing left was to eat it.

Along with our pork chops (there was fresh meat all over the front lines that day—we met pork chops in several places) we had dehydrated potatoes served mashed with gravy, canned peas, canned beets, fruit-salad mixture, marmalade, butter, and a sheet of sugar buns. When we were ready for dessert we were served a sheet of cherry pie.

Captain Ernest had the same pride in the morale of his bakers that a front-line commander has in the courage of his troops. "Our boys really began to work when they put us down here on Highway Six where we were within sound of guns. In Africa we were much farther behind the lines. Hearing those guns did something to the boys. They put up the equipment and started operating in record time."

I could watch the operations from where we sat, under our open tent half. Loaves by the hundreds were being wheeled in racks in a steady stream from the bakery tent, placed in covers of mattress ticking, and loaded on QM trucks. Forty-eight thousand pounds of bread, I was told, were produced every twenty-four hours.

No flight commander has ever been prouder of the heroism of his fliers than the Captain of the record of his unit. "And they keep on breaking more records all the time," he told me.

The last evidence of record breaking came in the form of a handsome inlaid plaque from General Clark. The citation accompanying it read:

> Often in the face of serious obstacles and always with un-
> swerving devotion to our supreme purpose of destroying the
> enemy, you have established an outstanding record in the per-
> formance of services invaluable to the Fifth Army. There are
> many difficult tasks before us but we know that victory will
> be ours. With confidence I shall rely upon the 110th Quarter-
> master Bakery Company to maintain its record in the days
> that lie ahead.

One of the tools of modern war is definitely the mobile bake oven.

After mess I took some pictures. "Boy, wait till our folks see our pictures in *Life!*" the bakers kept exclaiming.

Remarks like these, which I repeatedly heard wherever I worked, always worried me, for I knew *Life* would have room to print only a small proportion of the many pictures I took. When we photographers are out on assignment, we cover the subject as thoroughly as possible and the complete series is sifted down in New York. Which pictures see print depends not necessarily on which are the best photographs, but which fit best into whatever editorial idea is being followed for the com- pleted picture story.

I mentioned this to Captain Ernest. "Never mind," he said. "It does the boys so much good to know that at last somebody has come to pay attention to them that they will be bucked up by this for weeks." And he went off with the ordnance officer to show him the camp layout.

T/5 Thurman S. Peedin, 30, of Princeton, N.C.: Combat engineer.

PHOTOGRAPH SECTION III. COMBAT ENGINEERS

Mines are everywhere. Hunting them is dangerous and undramatic, but the Army cannot move ahead while they remain hidden.

Private Elmer Kuhlman (in overcoat), 23, of Denison, Iowa, and Private
Edwardo Martinez, 32, of Brickettsville, Texas.

A mine is a mutilating weapon. Mine hunters' casualties are among the highest in the Army. The job is most nerve-racking, and these men have been doing it for four hours.

This is called a "beehive" and contains a charge of TNT.

Armies have to have roads. This enormous boulder was toppled into the road by the Germans, and the engineers are setting a charge to blast it out of the way.

A bigger bridge will follow. This one permits infantry to keep on the heels of the enemy.

This was a troublesome bridge. The Volturno in flood washed it out three times.

It was built to pass combat traffic.

PFC Ivan B. Harvey, 25, of Greenwood, Texas, bridge corpsman.
Drove a truck before the war.

First Lieutenant Tom Farrell, 23, of Albany, N.Y. West Pointer, son of Colonel Farrell, chief engineer of the American forces in India. Decorated. Died at Anzio.

Fra Mario, known as "Friar Tuck." His great secret: plenty of garlic.

Morning in the monastery courtyard. Fra Antonio (with friend) was known as "KP" because he helped in the kitchen.

Sergeant Berthold L. Sadkins is studying aerial photographs of enemy-held territory to determine how much material needs to be brought up to repair demolished bridges as soon as we have taken the territory. In New York, his home, Sadkins won first prize for a United China Relief Poster.

German demolition.

The rubber pontoon is a bridge corps' donkey.

When I finished taking pictures I turned to the group of GI's that surrounded me. "Now," I said, "let me ask you a few questions." And I plunged in. "What are you fighting for?"

"Funny you should ask us that," said the top sergeant. "We had an essay contest about that just a while ago."

"Tell her about the winning essay," said the others, chuckling.

"Well, the men were asked to write a composition as lengthy as could be. The subject: 'Why I'm Fighting.' The winning composition was very short—just six words: 'Why I'm fighting. I was drafted.' "

"Some essay," laughed the boys.

"O.K.," I said. "Now tell me in more than six words."

"To get home," said one of the boys.

"That's only three," I prodded.

"Because Germany has a different form of government," said a second.

"To protect our homes and our country," volunteered a third.

"So we can get the war over quick and go home," was the fourth contribution.

"Do you want to find things at home exactly the way you left them?" I asked. The answer to this one was easy. A chorus of voices assured me that merely getting home was all any man could ask.

As they talked, I wished that people back in America could hear about the perfection their boys expected to return to. These soldiers had had a lot of time to remember what their homeland was like, and the memory seemed to them beyond improvement.

The top sergeant summed it up. "Yes, being over here has certainly taught us to appreciate America. It has really made us more patriotic. We've seen the poor Ayrabs, and we know how they live. We've seen the poor Eyetalians, and they don't even have shower baths."

"All right," I said. "You're fighting for shower baths. In the last war there was a well-worn slogan about what everybody was fighting for. Anything like that this time?"

"But, the last time, at the end of World War I, the soldier got a terrible dirty deal," said a baby-faced lad with POPS lettered on his cap.

"Believe me, here's one soldier who intends to see there will be no breadline this time," said the top sergeant.

"What can be done to prevent it?" I asked.

"Well, a college education for one thing," said Pops. "Maybe we

could get a year's college with fifty dollars a month for expenses, an
all our textbooks."

"Yes," said a freckled PFC they called Red. "Lots of us are just ou
of high school. We expect to be taught to make a good living becaus
most of us never held a real job before. We really expect the govern
ment to have something planned for us. We're so used to having thing
planned for us that most of us wouldn't know which way to turn on ou
own."

When the talk drifted to agitation for the soldiers' vote, Pops re
marked, "Well, we figure that's a gesture of gratitude from the folk
back home. It's a link with the home town. You don't get your mai
regular, sometimes, and you like to hear about the home folks going t
so much trouble to get something for you."

"Don't you think who gets elected may have something to do witl
how the country is run?" I ventured.

"Well, maybe so. It's just like me paying my electricity bill," sai
Pops. "I figure that we pay a salary to some guy that runs the electrica
company, and that's what I figure we have representatives of the peopl
in the government for."

The top sergeant, however, took a much more positive stand. "Ther
shouldn't have to be any legislation made, and argued, so that we cai
vote—it should be understood and automatic. When men leave thei
country, give up their jobs, leave their homes, and sometimes even sac
rifice their lives to preserve the democratic way of life, why anyone cai
question this right to vote is beyond me."

We were joined in the middle of this discussion by two exceptionall
tall, exceptionally lean fellows who both spoke in the same soft Louisi
ana drawl. The sandy-haired one was called Slats, and the one with ;
premature bald spot was Spike.

"You two guys have never been known to agree about anything yet,
said the top sergeant. "We're talking about democracy and the soldiers
vote. It seems to me that if a man fights for democracy he should a
least be able to participate in it. If this is to be a democracy, everyon
should have the chance to vote."

"But something *must* be done to curb the Negro vote in the South,
Slats advanced emphatically. "I'm not too strong on racial prejudice
but if the Negroes are allowed the same vote as white people, it won't b

very many years until they'll control the South, and in their present condition they have no business being in executive positions."

"It's quite a paradox," Spike broke in, "that we're fighting for democracy and yet the South is upset about the Negro vote. Too bad—though personally I don't care for Negroes any more than the next man."

"It's a stunt that was pulled on us while we were over here! That's what it is," Slats reported heatedly.

The top sergeant smiled. "See, I told you they'd never agree," he said.

"Well, if the Supreme Court has ruled that Negroes can vote in the primaries, that's all right with me," Spike said quietly. "The bad part of it is that a lot of dirty politicians will take advantage of their ignorant ideas."

"The whole thing is a bad move," Slats asserted. "Believe me, we over here ought to know if anybody does. The Negro in the Army is hard to control." Slats was becoming excited.

"They might be a little better if they had had enough education to know what the score is," said Spike, again speaking calmly.

"But the real thing that gets us hot under the collar is some of those political geniuses in Congress," volunteered Red, changing the subject.

"I've heard more than one man say he'd like to lay his hands on some of those characters," Pops remarked. "Those stupid Congressmen that said three hundred dollars or four hundred dollars was too much for us. And you can take it from me they weren't kidding. But this mustering-out pay isn't even a beginning."

"As far as the government aiding us after the war," said Slats, "we're mighty skeptical. Practically anything the government tries to do for us after this thing is over, we'll have to pay for in taxes to keep it going."

"What really makes the fellows sore," said Red, "is all the talk about getting sent home, and nobody seems to know anything about it. Like being promised a raise and never getting it."

"That's really a bitter line," Slats said. "The only reason they're sending a few home is for the benefit of the home front."

"The American soldier in this theater," the top sergeant said, "and I think I speak for practically all of them, wants to see the States again before going elsewhere. We've had all this experience now so we're all of us afraid that they're going to send us on to India or someplace. But there's plenty of fellows back in training camps might as well get some experience. We'll never understand the why of it if they're going to send us from here directly to the other half of the war."

"It wouldn't be so bad if only we had something to look forward to," said Red. "The way it is now there doesn't seem to be any hope of getting home before the war is over."

Slats was warming to the new subject. "And maybe not then," he said. "It's going to end up with their releasing those John Does that had maybe a year's service, all in the States. And those who have fought the war over here staying on afterwards as troops of occupation, and probably having three or four years' service. Well, this should be turned around. But I'll bet my last dollar that it ain't."

There was no doubt that these men felt a deep insecurity about their future in civilian life. They were worried about whether women in industry would be willing to hand their jobs back. They were deeply resentful toward organized labor without having much information about the issues. They felt they had a score to settle with those people who, while the boys were overseas, had been home "feathering their own nests."

Pops sized it up, "We often wonder if this just won't end up like the last war, a big grab by everyone."

"It isn't so much cash that the men want," the top sergeant concluded, as Padgitt and I began to gather up the cameras and place them in the jeep. "It's a job—a good job—with enough pay so we can buy a home, an automobile, and raise a family. Is that too much to ask?"

The question-and-answer program came to a halt with the return of Captain Ernest and the ordnance officer. My traveling companion was eager to get me on to a heavy maintenance depot, where a gun-tube change was in process. "Get some of that Swedish pastry for them to eat on the way," said Captain Ernest; so, loaded with a sheet of pastry still warm from the oven, we started toward the Ordnance Depot.

When we drove into the grove which had been taken over by the Heavy Maintenance Ordnance Company my first reaction was: how very American. Then I decided that only from the knees up was it American; from the knees down this could only be muddy Italy. Slithering back and forth through a lake of chocolate sauce were mobile units of giant machinery. Dozens of GI's slogged through their tasks with the precision of machinists on the concrete floor of an American factory.

When the tube-changing operation on the fifteen-ton Long Tom started, it looked like a meeting of dinosaurs. Heavy wreckers with long-necked cranes sparred and maneuvered through the mud. One eight-wheeled wrecker with an enormous boom backed up to the gun and the boom was hooked to the worn-out gun barrel. A second wrecker edged its way up, until its winch was in position to ease the great gun carriage forward. When the old tube had been extracted, the new one, as long as a telephone pole, and weighing 9500 pounds, was lifted into the air. To act as counterbalance for the heavy breech end while the tube was being lowered into place, a group of men jumped up and sat astride the muzzle end of the gun like a row of schoolboys on a seesaw.

As the gun tube was finally eased onto the carriage, the human ballast jumped down to talk to me. It made me feel a bit self-conscious to go about all day asking soldiers what they were fighting for, but I was interested, so once more I plunged in.

A broad-shouldered master sergeant with ACE lettered on his helmet replied, "I don't suppose there's any man here would want to leave till it was all over and done with, but most of us want to get this mess cleaned up and go home."

"I suppose a lot of us are fighting for our wives and kids," said the pug-nosed test recorder.

"Hey, Bud, maybe you got kids," said Ace, "but I happen to know you ain't got no wife."

"Well, I can dream, can't I?" remarked Bud. "There's approximately forty million girls in America and all of them can't be smart."

"I guess there's lots of fellows fighting for babies they haven't seen," said the winch operator.

"That's my case," remarked a small-arms inspector. "The way my wife writes, she seems to expect our kid to talk, creep, and have teeth all at two months and six days. I tell her she must think she's got Superman, Jr."

"Write her to watch out or the draft board will be calling him for an interview," chuckled Bud.

"I'm one guy that's twice as bad off," said Ace, and the others laughed because Ace had recently become the father of twins.

"All right," I said. "You're fighting for the babies you have or the babies you hope to have. Anything else?"

"I can tell you what we ain't fighting for," volunteered an auburn-haired PFC they called Ruby. "We ain't fighting for none of those labor leaders."

"That's right," said the winch operator. "Let some of those jokers hear a few screaming meemies come whistling at them and they'd be glad to go back down into a nice deep coal mine."

"I know a lot of fellows that are going to react like that soldier we heard of that punched John L.'s face when he got back to the States," said Ruby.

"And another thing," put in the winch operator. "The government is going to have to aid the veterans, especially the wounded. I know what some men have given up, and the government and citizens owe it to these fellows to re-establish them. If all sorts of aid isn't given to veterans, there's going to be plenty of trouble, and you can quote me on that."

"On the subject of veterans," said Ace. "There should be a New Veterans of Foreign Wars organized."

This was a subject I had heard broached before, and it seemed to me a constructive step to find some soldiers thinking about it.

"We shouldn't be swept up by the old organization of veterans who would get us a bonus of five hundred or a thousand dollars and say, 'See what we got for you,'" continued Ace. "The men who fought this war should be the ones to have a hand in things, and see that returning soldiers don't get kicked around. The New Veterans should be run by men who went through this war. And they should be organized so they can keep an eye on political legislation."

"That sounds like a step in the right direction," I said. "With the right leadership they could accomplish a great deal."

"I feel that the better the aid for veterans, the easier the rehabilitation and reconstruction," Ace went on. "It isn't that I think our country owes us anything. What we're doing we're doing for ourselves and our loved ones and the right to live in a country like ours."

"How about most of the men you know over here?" I asked. "Does the average man do much thinking about whether there's a connection between our war aims and getting rid of Fascism?"

The small-arms inspector had been listening attentively and at this point he broke in with: "I don't think that's a subject for the average American to think about."

Just then my ordnance guide returned to tell me that he wanted to show me one more installation before nightfall. The boys called, "Good luck; come back some time and take more pictures," and we were on our way.

"That was interesting," Padgitt commented.

I had found the final statement of the small-arms inspector the most interesting of all. Why was it, I wondered, that the "average American" both in and out of the Army shrank from digging into the issues of this war when they concerned him so deeply. Some of them, like Ace, evidently had given the problem thought, but it was not the rule. I knew from my previous experience during the Russian war that all you had to do was to give the average Russian an opening and he would break into impassioned oratory on the subject. He would trace all the relationships as he saw them among book burnings, oppression of minorities, racial injustice, and war. The average Britisher would make shorter speeches, but would discuss articulately the issues of war and international politics. Even in Chungking, I had heard thoughtful and comprehensive opinions expressed by the Chinese.

And yet we were so clever and quick about everything else. The bakery and the heavy maintenance ordnance unit I had seen that day were two of the countless expert activities which make ours the best-fed and best-equipped army in the world. The same organizing ability which enabled us to establish hotel chains, bakery companies, mailorder houses, transportation and maintenance facilities to serve and supply our great territory of forty-eight states was being translated effectively into the organization of war. Maybe our accomplishments had made us smug.

Our jeep came to a stop as the road dipped into a stream bed. A line of trucks spaced far back on the road was waiting to ford the stream. As we waited our turn, I noticed that a dead mule, which blocked a rivulet beside us, had built up its own little dam of muddy water. A large truck full of GI's started plunging across the flooded road. It got stuck in the middle and it took some time for the driver, with the help of a road gang, to negotiate the ford. This gave me an opportunity to study the faces of the human cargo the truck carried.

They were infantrymen returning to a bivouac area for rest, and I knew from the division emblem they wore on their sleeves that these men had been up in the mountains around Cassino for an unbroken sixty days.

I thought I had never seen such tired faces. It was more than the stubble of beard that told the story; it was the blank, staring eyes. The men were so tired that it was like a living death. They had come from such a depth of weariness that I wondered if they would ever be able quite to make the return to the lives and thoughts they had known.

I had talked with Army medical men about such infantry soldiers returning from battle, and I knew that some of them would have temporarily lost their ability to sleep or to hear. It would be a long time before some of them would be able to listen to even a friendly plane overhead without cringing; and sudden sharp noises would make many of them jump for the rest of their lives.

Later, when their truck carried them farther away from the battle, their spirits would pick up and most of them would begin to laugh and joke, as GI's always manage to do. They would file into that blessed shower bath which the delousing unit had established, and when they emerged, all clean and dripping, they would be handed clean clothes and given haircuts and shaves. But now their front-line experience was too close for GI jokes, and they were too tired.

It was ironical the way a prewar road sign, sticking out of a puddle not far from the fallen mule, still pointed to Cassino. As though all you had to do was to follow the road to get there. The men in the truck had been trying to get there, and now that they were coming back they seemed to be returning from a land too far away for most of us to see— so far away that it was beyond all those sane and normal things which men hold dear.

When the big truck finally extricated itself from the stream, and the MP in charge waved us across, Padgitt said, "One of my buddies from Des Moines just came back from there. He told me if you could dry out your boots you could stand it. Two months running, up there, and you can't ever get your feet dry."

We drove on through the deepening dusk, with the guns spurting jagged flashes from every muddy glen and gully. I tried to imagine living for sixty days without once getting your shoes dry. It seemed to me that only one thing would make it possible to bear sixty days in soaking boots, sixty days of near-misses from screaming shells, and that was a support which many of these men did not have. The only way the human spirit could endure such torture unscathed was the deep, glowing knowledge of what the fight was for.

CHAPTER 9

The Eyes of the Artillery

ON THE EDGE of a large airfield with Mt. Vesuvius forming a smoking background is a row of identical little buildings looking somewhat like overgrown chicken coops. Close by they take on a resemblance to squatters' houses. Inside they are filled with welding tools, improvised desks, cots, and footlockers, and they are inhabited by mechanics and pilots of the Grasshopper Squadron. These curious examples of war architecture are the packing crates in which the Cubs, folded up like dismembered dragonflies, arrive from America. Since shelter is always a problem in wartime, the artillery liaison pilots turn the crate in which each new Cub arrives into a workshop or a billet.

In one of these Lieutenant Michael Strok, Engineering Officer for the artillery liaison pilots, had his office. I had met Mike some weeks before I came to Italy at an airfield in North Africa where I was waiting for flying weather. On the basis of our being fellow Cornellians, Mike had come up and introduced himself and invited me to a pilots' dance. Mike jitterbugged like the college kid he had so recently been. But I discovered that evening, during those brief moments in swing when a minimum of conversation is possible, that Mike would rave even on the dance floor about his beloved Grasshopper planes.

Mike was one of the original handful of men who had faith in the possibilities of the flying observation post as an adjunct to artillery effectiveness, and who worked against distrust and opposition, at the beginning of the war, until the liaison planes proved themselves in trial by combat.

He had that nervous, sensitive face which is typical of pilots or crusaders—and Mike Strok was both. The slight twitch in his left eye added to his constant expression of great eagerness. He was a Cornell graduate, class of '38, his father was a technical assistant in the Physics Department at Cornell, and his younger sister was studying to be a pilot, too.

Since the air OP's do not belong to the Air Force, but are part of artillery, and since their work is one of the newest developments of this war, Lieutenant Strok had had to use considerable ingenuity to devise maintenance facilities. He had adapted routine Army equipment to the special needs of Cubs. Standard 6x6 trailers had been fitted up with welding apparatus and hydraulic presses so that they could be driven to the forward landing strips where repair and maintenance could be carried on right behind the front. On these improvised air bases, as I saw in the case of Captain Marinelli, most of the servicing was done by the fliers themselves; never was there more than one ground mechanic, and he frequently doubled as flying observer; and the pilots often did their own cooking.

From the very beginning, the tiny observation planes had to earn their way. On the first day of the North African invasion, when on November 8, 1942, three Pipers took off from an aircraft carrier, they began running into difficulties. Headed toward the mainland at an altitude of 600 feet, they were fired on by a group of Navy vessels who did not recognize them as friendly planes, having never seen our Army use Cubs before.

Dodging to a level just above the water, they made for the beach, where they were immediately fired on by our infantry troops, who had been catching frequent punishment from French strafing planes. Two of the Cubs managed to land safely, and they were the first American planes to land in Africa at the beginning of the invasion; but the third Cub was shot down, crashed, and burned. Its pilot, Captain Alcorn, was hit in the legs by machine-gun bullets. His fellow Cub pilots were in great distress, fearing he would lose his legs; but he recovered and was sent home to train other pilots at Fort Sill to do air reconnaissance work.

After that first unfortunate trial, it took quite a while before the Piper pilots were given a second chance. In the beginning our artillery commanders didn't know how to use the Cubs, and the pilots didn't know much more since they arrived with only schoolbook tactics. They had been taught to fly only behind our own guns and never at a higher altitude than 600 feet.

Since then the tactics manual has been thrown away. Pilots fly forward of our guns, over no man's land when it is needed, rise to any necessary altitude, and go directly over the enemy lines when the mission requires it. On night missions they soar up to a height of 7000 feet.

In the face of considerable skepticism on the part of the Air Force, who were conditioned to larger, faster planes, the adoption of Cubs by the Army for air liaison was due largely to Brigadier General Thomas Edward Lewis, Artillery Officer with General Mark Clark's staff.

"When we didn't have them, we didn't miss them," General Lewis told me. "But now we have them we couldn't do without them."

Bulletheaded, energetic little Tom Lewis is a West Pointer from San Antonio. "Born and raised in artillery," as he expresses it, he proceeded on the firm belief that the planes which observed for Army artillery should be an integral part of artillery, not a detached group under the Air Force. This attitude has not always pleased some of the more traditional Air Force officers, who feel that enough observing can be done by the Air Force on the side to keep the artillery boys happy. But it has greatly pleased Mark Clark, who is thoroughly sold on the little planes as a means of increasing the accuracy of artillery fire. General Clark often flies in Cubs, and the Grasshoppers have also flown General Eisenhower.

From these slow-flying planes, the whole military picture is spread out like a map. Therefore, one of the uses of the Cub is to fly a unit commander who may want to look down and see the deployment of his troops, inspect camouflage, and check the location and disposition of his guns. Sometimes, too, the Cub will fly courier missions for the quick transportation of vital orders necessary in an army chain of command.

However, the main duties of the Grasshoppers are adjustment of fire, surveillance, and reconnaissance. As flying liaison with artillery, there is no limit to their fire power. One Cub in one day can bring down as much destruction as a squadron of bombing planes. In some artillery units, eighty-five per cent of the observation has been by air. Slow, low-flying planes are ideal for this. They may be Taylor Craft, but the majority in use are Piper Cubs. In Army terminology, they are the eyes of the artillery.

The assignment that the Grasshopper pilots like best is to go out searching for "targets of opportunity." They are delighted when they spot a traffic jam. This may occur when German trucks with food supplies or armored carriers moving troops strike a narrow bridge or bottleneck. It makes the Grasshopper pilot very happy to go buzzing about overhead, just above small-arms range, radioing back to the gun crews who will start plastering the area before the swastika-painted motor vehicles can escape.

Sometimes they have unusual missions, such as dropping propaganda leaflets by moonlight, or coming to the rescue of our own marooned troops. Once above Venafro some infantry were cut off in a region too steep for even mules to reach. For a time they had been supplied by a human conveyor line for which soldiers climbed the slopes and passed rations up from shoulder to shoulder. At last an encircling action by the enemy cut off even this tenuous supply belt.

It was not easy for the Cub to drop rations, since the tiny plane is not designed to carry a load. Lieutenant Strok took a bomb shackle, designed a release mechanism, and made drop tests on the field. Then the Cub flew off to deliver forty pounds of rations.

The trapped soldiers were near the summit of a bowl-shaped mountain 4000 feet high, which meant rough air for the little plane. They had dug in only twenty yards below the crest of the ridge. The Cub had to keep below the mountaintop while dropping its rations because if seen by the Germans, who were just on the other side, it would draw fire not only on the plane but on the boys who were concealed below the crest. The job was difficult, but carried through successfully.

The next day the Cub returned to the trapped soldiers with machine-gun parts, which were dropped in a sack attached to a paratrooper's parachute. Within forty minutes the boys below had it assembled and firing toward the enemy. The next day the Cub dropped litters for the wounded, and from then on, every day for two weeks, the Piper returned, depositing its forty pounds of food and water until a forward move on the front lines released the troops from their trap.*

The Piper Cub is nothing but a fragile bundle of feather-light tubing and canvas, highly inflammable, and vulnerable to ground fire as well as enemy aircraft. Considerations of lightness and flexibility have kept it unarmed and unarmored. When a pilot is attacked he escapes by his wits.

Sometimes the very slowness of these planes acts as a protection. (Relative slowness was also a defense mechanism of the Russian Stormovik.) A hair-raising example of this occurred with a pilot I knew who was meandering at a leisurely pace, following the curve of a hill. Sud-

---

* On subsequent missions of this kind, regulation army blankets have been used as parachutes, so that the 'chute itself is a useful article when it reaches the ground.

denly a Messerschmitt headed around the mountain behind him. I guess the Messerschmitt was almost as surprised as he was.

The relative speed of the Cub was so much slower than that of the fighter that it threw the Nazi pilot off his aim. In a breath he was so close that his guns were converging ahead of the Cub instead of in it. The startled Cub pilot found a stream of tracer bullets pouring on each side of his plane.

This was pretty devastating but not so bad as if this lead had been converging in the cockpit. These gleaming rows of machine-gun bullets passing on either side of the fuselage sawed off both wings. The pilot rolled over, tumbled out in his parachute, and escaped with his life.

Another boy made an even more miraculous escape when he was attacked by six Messerschmitts. He went into a snap roll and maneuvered so low that he almost shook the attackers, but in a parting shot the last Jerry plane got him through the tail and set his plane on fire. Too low to use a parachute, he did the only thing he could do. He put his flaming plane into a steep dive and crash-landed. Everything would have worked out splendidly if he hadn't had the bad luck to hit a slit trench. It rolled the plane over on its back. The pilot was thrown out, and the plane exploded.

When he pulled himself together he realized that not only had he lost his plane, but several teeth as well. However, there were no further injuries and he didn't seem to mind having paid with his teeth for the record of being the only Piper pilot who escaped half a dozen Messerschmitts at once.

Once a couple of Piper Cubs managed to lure seven Messerschmitts to their destruction. The enemy had temporarily stopped attacking Spitfires because their losses had been too heavy, but they were lying in wait for the unarmored Cubs wherever they could find them. We knew this, and one day while a formation of Spitfires hung behind a mountain two Cubs went up to act as bait.

They flew in leisurely circles until a flock of Messerschmitts appeared and chased them. The Pipers dived low and immediately our Spitfires came over the mountain and tangled with the Messerschmitts before they had time to turn and run. It cost the Germans all seven Messerschmitts.

Only because we owned the air above southern Italy were we able to use these defenseless Cubs with such efficiency. The Germans also attempted to use air OP's. Two of them were shot down near Mignano.

The Nazis had copied one of our older planes, the O-49, in their Feisler Storch—a high-wing job with lots of glass. Our pilots consider it a good plane but too unwieldy to land on roads or manhandle the way we do our Cubs. In any event, partly because of their inferior equipment and partly for lack of control of the air, the German air OP's have been less efficient.

The British make considerable use of air OP's, also. Theirs is a one-seater model larger and heavier than our Cub, as it bears light armor, a protection our boys are willing to forgo in order to have room for an observer, and for the sake of superior maneuverability.

We were all puzzled, during the time our engineers were working on the Ponte Reale bridge below Venafro, by the frequent appearance of a Cub with stars painted on both wings, instead of on one, in the regulation manner. Our antiaircraft crews hesitated to shoot at it until we had had a chance to find out more about it. It seemed as though it couldn't be a coincidence that frequently after its visits a Nazi strafing plane appeared within the hour. However, just as our Piper pilots had planned a trap so they could waylay this plane in the air and get a close look at the pilot, the mystery Cub disappeared, never to return again.

The Grasshoppers have received their most valued testimonials from the Germans themselves. In direct proportion to the almost personal affection with which our infantrymen regard the gallant little plane hedgehopping ahead of them toward the enemy, the German infantrymen have a personal hatred. Prisoners have been brought in raving about *der eisene Heinrich,* the iron Henry. "It's infuriating," they say, "to see that cursed little box floating back and forth, back and forth. Every time we make a move all hell breaks loose."

The Germans have become so cautious about revealing their gun positions when Piper Cubs are aloft that one of the reconnaissance pilots, Captain John Oswalt, decided to try to spot Nazi gun positions at night. Captain Oswalt chose a night when the moon was full, to take off in the Cub which his little sister had appropriately named the *Supersnooper.*

He flew at 5000 feet by prearrangement with our gun crews, not wanting to be shot down by our own side. In the bright moonlight he began crisscrossing over the region around Cassino. Spotting gun positions accurately at night would have been impossible if he had not flown over the valley so frequently that every road, town, house, and hillside was engraved on his brain.

"You can pick up moonlight against anything that is light," he explained to me, "rivers, the sides of houses, rocky cliffs. If you can get the moon in back of you, you can even see vehicles on the roads." He described how he picked out the gun flashes. The German gun positions around Cassino, he said, looked like a cloud of fireflies. After he had directed fire so as to knock out two German batteries he managed to find a tank for which Cub pilots had been searching unsuccessfully in the daytime, and called down fire to destroy that also. When the moon started sinking, he returned to the field only to find that the long shadow of a hill lay across his landing strip. The boys below had dared to mark the field only with a couple of C-ration cans filled with lighted gasoline, so Captain Oswalt came down over his landing strip, picking out his way, leaning out of his plane and directing his small flashlight toward the ground.

The *Supersnooper*'s pilot was typical of Grasshopper pilots, who are a highly educated, technically trained group. Captain Oswalt was twenty-four years old, a dapper-looking young man, with a tiny black mustache. Before his pilot days he had studied at Purdue University with the intention of becoming a mathematics professor.

The CO of the Grasshopper group, handsome Major John T. Walker, thirty-one years old, had been aviation editor of the *Springfield State Journal,* of Springfield, Illinois. During his work with the paper, and later as publicity director for the state of Illinois, he flew his own Piper Cub.

I found among the Piper Cub pilots nothing of the numbness, the cloying homesickness, the depressing waiting without defined objectives and without a vision of their contribution to the basic scheme of battle, which were unfortunately too apparent in many other branches of the Army. These boys knew they were pioneering. They had faith in the value of their work. This in itself gave them a remarkable morale. Their high spirit was none the less evident despite the peculiar circumstances under which many of them had to work: those who were trained overseas when the use of Cubs was rapidly expanding had no rating and consequently, even though they frequently flew as many as five missions a day, received no flying pay. In spite of their wealth of combat experience, some of them have even had to return to America to go to school before they could receive their rating.

New artillery observation pilots are being trained constantly. Several veterans have returned to instruct these, and among them is a Mormon missionary, Captain "Wild Bill" Cummings from Salt Lake City. When I saw him in Naples, he had just been awarded the DSC for taking off from an improvised runway on the deck of an LST "under incessant fire, and with utter disregard for personal safety, to spot and report positions of enemy artillery."

This he accomplished in a plane named *Maggie the Faithful* which made Grasshopper history. *Maggie the Faithful* was the first plane to take off during the invasion of Sicily. She was a veteran of the North African invasion and the Tunisian, Sicilian, and Italian campaigns. During these actions, she had flown 760 hours. She had received two sets of wings, and a new tail; a new engine and landing gear had been installed, and her propellers had been changed seven times. Even in this long record of service old age never caught up with her, but a severe windstorm finally did, and *Maggie the Faithful,* reputably battered, was farmed out to pasture.

Throughout my five months at the Italian front, the Grasshoppers flew me frequently over various war-torn areas. Although previously I had done a great deal of airplane photography, never before had I had the chance to hang out of a glass birdcage with complete vision of earth and sky. The ease with which my pilot hovered over any spot I selected made me feel I could almost have taken time exposures from the air.

We used to find odd things, puttering along at tree top level. Once we followed the splendid oil-pipe line through which the Army Service Forces pumped fuel direct from tankers in Naples Harbor to a supply point just behind Fifth Army lines. Over rivers, between hills, and through bombed fields ran this continuous line of slender piping, as inconspicuous as it was strategically important. At one point it crossed a shell-torn meadow, whitening with skeletons. These were not of men but of cattle unlucky enough to have been caught between the clash of armies. Farther forward it ran over the deep bomb craters of an abandoned airdrome, where Junker 88's, Messerschmitt 109's and Heinkel 111's littered the ground. Below us, these German planes lay dismembered as though a thoughtless schoolboy had picked flies apart, pulling off legs and wings with the unconscious cruelty of childhood, and scattering them.

One day, Lieutenant Strok flew me out over the Mediterranean and we swooped down to join a fleet of fishing boats, where we were prac-

Quick patch for war-zone roads: the Bailey Bridge, a great wartime invention.

PHOTOGRAPH SECTION IV. BAILEY BRIDGE

It goes together like a Meccano set—but with more grunting.

Fifty men doing fifty things—each in precise order.

Built on one side, the bridge is pushed across the river by **manpower**.

Cleaning up with dynamite.

Waiting for this bridge were supplies for two divisions.

8:30 A.M. to 3 P.M.—locking the bridge in place.

Finished in 6½ hours, the bridge makes a fine splint. Looks like it had been born there.

tically treading water, and so close above the surface that we seemed on a level with the rowers themselves.

Another day we explored Mt. Vesuvius. Lieutenant Strok flew me slowly around the mountain; in spiral fashion we would make our way higher and higher toward the edge of the crater. There were times when I could have leaned out and almost touched the solidified, black lava streams below.

The Lieutenant had hoped to give me a peek into the boiling crater itself. Whether or not we could do this depended on the air streams, and the only way to judge those was to go up and find out. As we climbed toward the top, the pillar of smoke which appeared as a neat white cloud from a distance took on an alarming grayish-mottled shape. Gusts of wind blew the pillar over us until we found ourselves flying through ever-darkening shadows. With the corrugated streams of ancient lava below, we seemed to be heading straight into Hades.

The light kept shifting, and the darkness grew deeper. Now we were closer to the serrated edge of the crater. A little more elevation, and we would be able to peep inside when suddenly a downdraft caught us with such fury that our Piper was almost thrown over on its back.

We were thrashed back and forth until once the heavy airplane camera I was holding hit me in the jaw with what seemed to me almost a knockout blow; but in a brief interval, as we were being tossed about, I was able to snatch a picture of the churning smoke rising just above us.

Lieutenant Strok did a magnificent job of handling his fragile aircraft, and soon he got us away from the volcano and out again into the sunlight. "I was afraid you would drop the camera," he shouted back over his shoulder.

"I have never dropped a camera yet," I said, "and I don't propose to begin by dropping cameras into Mt. Vesuvius."

CHAPTER 10

Cloak-and-Dagger Men

I OFTEN WONDERED what the Marchesa would have thought if she could have seen the procession of mud-caked characters on leave from the front who used her pink and crystal bath. I believe my appearance would have surprised her most of all. In my GI pants and knee-length leggings, my enormous boots filled out with several pairs of wool socks, my peaked pilot's cap which the Grasshopper boys had given me, and my indescribably streaked and muddy trench coat, I must have represented a most unappetizing example of womanhood.

I have no way of knowing how many splendid bathrooms may have brightened the lives of Neapolitans before the air raids. But without doubt, the Marchesa's was the finest to remain intact after the bombings. It looked like Hollywood's idea of what the bathroom of a marchesa should be.

Many American officers who had hitherto spent their lives amidst Grand Rapids furniture and typical American home and office architecture found themselves in exotic new surroundings. Some even worked in palaces. This is due to the Army practice of requisitioning with each new occupation of territory any buildings which may be of use for headquarters, offices, or billets. The civilian owners are paid rent, and their buildings are returned to them when the Army moves on.

The Marchesa's magnificent bath was the accidental acquisition of the Counter-Intelligence Corps. When they requisitioned her trembling old apartment, one of the few buildings still standing in a partly wrecked block, they found that deep in a maze of marble halls and behind glass doors as big as shopwindows was something the like of which no American officer had ever seen. I don't think even the colored pages of *The Ladies' Home Journal* had ever reflected such a tasteful blending of rose-veined marble, such profusion of cutglass fittings, such splendor of mirrors and crystal.

90

However, it was not the pink marble that attracted all the muddy visitors returning on leave who could wangle an invitation from Counter-Intelligence. It was the fact that by some freak, even after the building had been knocked almost dizzy from near-by bomb hits, the Marchesa's water pipes still continued to furnish hot running water.

It was not only their fabulous bath that was unusual about the Counter-Intelligence Corps. They were in some ways the most remarkable group in the Army. In private life most of the members had been either legal investigators, college professors, newspaper men, musicians, and even missionaries' children. The presence of missionaries is due to their knowledge of languages. In the entire corps, seventy different languages are spoken; some members know as many as a dozen apiece. Many of them can master any new language they need in from four to six weeks. Within their relatively small personnel they represent the faculties of fifty American universities. They include men trained in every branch of the Army, who must pass as experts in their field: Artillery, Air Corps, Engineering, and so on. Like the Rangers and the Paratroopers, the Counter-Intelligence Corps is a voluntary organization. In 1917 a corp of intelligence police was formed, but it never became very sizable. Its present counterpart grew rapidly after Pearl Harbor.

Differing from Intelligence, which exists for the purpose of getting information, the job of Counter-Intelligence is to prevent information from reaching the enemy. The corps is responsible for the security of our troops.

The beautiful blond spy is unfortunately a rarity these days, the Counter-Intelligence boys will tell you, but it is their job to catch espionage agents, most of whom are less glamorous than the spy of fiction. In a terrain like Italy, where slipping across the lines is not too difficult, and where the enemy has had the advantage of previous occupation to lay his espionage lines, the trapping of spies takes operators who have been trained for it. "Just a group of cloak-and-dagger men," they will tell you.

To the Army, the Counter-Intelligence Corps is known as CIC. To the Italians it is Cheech. If you asked a Counter-Intelligence character what CIC stood for, his reply would depend on his mood. He might say, "Commandos in Chairs," or "Christ, it's confused."

CIC men are on the spot wherever our troops go, to make sure our fighting men are not stabbed in the back. They guard against sabotage and subverrsive acts. Some members operate far behind the lines, taking charge of harbor security, preventing Fascist rings from organizing against the Allies. Others work at the front, sometimes actually going in ahead of our infantry. Working as intimately as they do with civilians, and seeing firsthand, as few in our Army have a chance to see, the effects of Fascism, the members are passionately and articulately anti-Fascist.

The men stationed in rear areas do a great deal of their work anonymously. Those who advance with our forward echelons into newly captured territory wear a conspicuous armband lettered CIC in red. This is so that civilians who are friendly to the Allies—and there are many of these in each new territory we wrest from the Nazis—will recognize "Cheech" and help to ferret out anti-Ally groups. As soon as a town is captured, CIC takes immediate possession of all communications centers, the railroad station and telephone exchanges. They investigate the mayor and all civic officials. They check all traffic so that no enemy agents can sift their way in or out.

In this, they work closely with our military police, who do the actual policing. Ordinary crimes, such as robbery or murder, are handled by the MP's. Any persons under suspicion of being active or passive agents of the enemy are handled by CIC.

The enemy has its counterpart; and by the very nature of their work, our organization and the enemy's know a good deal about each other. Our officers know their opposite numbers in the German army. They may have five or six names for the same individual and not know which is the right one, but they know he exists. It is a good deal the way airmen in the last war often knew the names and personal characteristics of the pilots against whom they flew.

My introduction to CIC's pink-marble bathroom came about in a peculiar way. Having returned disheveled from one of my trips to the front, I was desperate for a shampoo. Hairdressers in Naples had either been bombed out or generally mislaid in the confusion. I happened to mention to a solemn, lantern-jawed lieutenant we called "Laughing Boy" how lovely it would be to get my hair waved. Previously a professor of romance languages at Tennessee's University of the South at Sewanee, he was now chief of investigations for CIC.

"You're just the person we need to vet Peppino," said Laughing Boy.

"What do you mean 'vet'?" I asked.

"Investigate," he replied.

"And who is Peppino?"

"Peppino is the waiter at our mess. We have to be particularly thorough about vetting waiters. Peppi seems all right; he claims to have been a hairdresser before the war. None of us is qualified to test that. Would you be able to tell?"

"Would I?" I said. "Lead me to the investigation. Peppino, here I come!"

There was one incongruous note in the astonishingly pink bathroom at the CIC billet, and that was the single towel. I suppose it was correct to refer to it as a towel, although it had long ceased to look like one. With each visitation of muddy officers it grew more frayed, more nondescript in hue, less recognizable as a towel. I am sure it would have deeply shocked the Marchesa, but, after all, CIC had not sent me there to investigate their towel.

Peppino handled everything. Suave, and very beauty-salonish with black lacquered hair, and wearing an apron bearing unmistakable traces of C rations, he took charge of the situation. I had forgotten that towels could be as white as the one he dug up from somewhere. And in addition he produced a charming beruffled bib that could only have come from the linen chest of the Marchesa.

With this embroidered bit of immaculate fluff tied on over my disreputable field jacket, he went to work. After dunking my head thoroughly under the Marchesa's shower, he even produced a drier. When it was over, I emerged from the pink marble so curled, swirled, and ringleted that I looked like a sculptured Assyrian bull.

"It seems to have been a successful investigation," said the CIC boys.

"Well," I said, "I'm not so sure."

"What do you mean? Only somebody who had done it from the cradle could put that many curls on a single head."

"Well, I'm new at this vetting business," I explained. "I'd hate to give you boys a wrong diagnosis. To be really sure of Peppino I think he should be vetted once a week. Or at least as often as I can make it back from the front."

So many CIC officers had been university instructors that they used to say that from their ranks they could set up a complete college faculty. And so many were musicians that they claimed they could make up an entire symphony orchestra. Those who were stationed in Naples, or who flowed back and forth between the front lines and the pink bathroom, had wonderful musical evenings. It took all the talent of a CIC investigator to get a melody out of the Marchesa's piano. Disuse and near-by bomb hits had played havoc with it. But when Julien sat down and started out on Massenet's *Elegy* or the Gershwin *Rhapsody in Blue,* the keys seemed to fall magically into tune.

Julien, a captain, had studied music in Paris and Vienna, and then had abandoned music for the United States State Department. As a member of our Consular Service, and later as an investigator for the U. S. Treasury, he has lived in most of the capitals of the world. His specialty is smuggling, particularly jewel smuggling. It is an oddity of war that international jewel smugglers tend to become espionage agents.

Plump little Julien, sitting smiling at the Marchesa's piano, is one of my vivid memories of Naples. He could accompany anybody; give Julien a snatch of melody and he would be right there. The Captain had several accomplished voices to accompany. The best singer, and incidentally the handsomest, was twenty-six-year-old Captain John Swarzwalder. Our favorite request number from John was the Schubert *Ave Maria,* which he sang beautifully, and his was really a fine voice. Captain Swarzwalder was an operatic baritone who had taught music at the University of Michigan. In the brighter spots of his career, he had sung opera; the more dubious periods he had devoted to burlesque. There was hardly a Jack's Place, Tom's Place, or Joe's Place in America where John had not sung, and when he reached the Pacific Coast he settled down for a term at the Sailor's Rendezvous. Here in Naples he was still covering the water front as Port Security Officer for G2.

CIC's other fine baritone was a Mormon missionary, and he was also tall, good-looking, and twenty-six. Second Lieutenant Smith, from Ogden, Utah, was an eager lad with an anxious curiosity about the world, and a nervous tick in his eye. Not only was Smitty a very good baritone; he was a very good boy. He had been brought up not to smoke and not to drink. But he was tolerant about these minor vices in others, and used to go graciously from glass to glass, pouring vino as we clustered around the piano.

Even CIC's commanding officer insisted that he could sing, although those of us who heard him shifting strangely from key to key were seldom inclined to agree with him.

"Oh, anybody can sing on one key," Pappy would protest. "I'm what is known as a four-key man."

Pappy was a good nickname for the CO, Major Maxwell Jerome Papurt, with his gray hair and wise bespectacled gaze making him look older than his thirty-six years. Like so many CIC officers, he had been a college professor—abnormal psychology, at Ohio State University. He was a specialist in the rehabilitation of the criminal, and he had served as consulting executive of many prisons and reformatories throughout the United States. He was a dead shot with a pistol, had great moral as well as physical courage, and commanded intense loyalty from his staff.

There were stories without number, most of which must remain secret until after the war, or perhaps forever, of how Pappy trapped a spy, sprang a booby trap, broke up an espionage ring. "Very cloak-and-daggerish," Pappy would say. For example: back in Africa a trap had been laid for some of his men. Saboteurs had set a flashing light in a window, to look as if someone were signaling enemy aircraft. A group of the boys started off to raid the building. Pappy, sensing that something was wrong, rushed there just in time to check his men from dashing through the building. Examining the door, he found a tripwire attached, and removed enough dynamite to have blown up most of his staff.

Our knot around the piano must have been the most strangely assorted group the Marchesa's ballroom had ever seen. But then the ballroom itself was a trifle strange. It was a vast cavern hung with yellow satin and glittering with gilt-edged mirrors. It was a freak that the mirrors had remained intact through the bombings, for the roof was literally falling in, and the cracked ceiling dripped plaster and wallpaper streamers like stalactites in a cave. It was so drafty and cold that we did most of our singing in overcoats. When it rained, a small waterfall splattered into the exact center of the ballroom. Peppino made a practice of keeping a dishpan in the middle of the floor. We all thought it would have been a fine place for goldfish, if we could have found any.

The ballroom had seemed even more cavernous in the early days in Naples before the power was turned on. Then the only source of light was a battered and incredibly branched and patched candelabra of the gilded cupid variety, set on a small glass table whose cracked top was also supported by gilt cupids. When the electricity went on the room was lighter, but it never got any warmer.

Sometimes the boys brought up nurses or Red Cross girls and we all danced, being careful not to trip on the Marchesa's inlaid floor, which was becoming as buckled and furrowed as a newly plowed field.

The best dancer in CIC was Smitty, the Mormon missionary, who was an accomplished jitterbug; and the second best was, oddly, another Mormon, newly arrived. He was a lieutenant named Gil, and he, unlike Smitty, occasionally took a sip of wine. Lieutenant Gil was the most soft-spoken, the shiest, the most modest officer in the CIC. Yet, curiously enough, whenever he dropped in for a dance during any of the musical evenings, it would always be with some lushly beautiful Italian girl. No one else was ever to see local girls who looked like this, much less get acquainted with them.

It was a great day in Naples when the Air Force took over the San Carlo Opera Company and opened the opera season with *La Bohème*. The house was jammed with enthusiastic soldiers, and CIC occupied a complete row. Smitty was so carried away that we were afraid he would jump on the stage and lend his voice to the rest. Between each act he wandered forward and consulted with the members of the orchestra. By the end of the performance he had arranged with the maestro to take singing lessons.

Although each number was noisily acclaimed by the appreciative hall full of GI's, some of the famous San Carlo singers seemed the worse for lack of practice and the undernourishment which inevitably grew out of war. But the leading role of Mimì, the flower girl, was superbly sung. I think Pina Esca was the plumpest Mimì ever to die to song. Although we did a good deal of kidding about how unconsumptive she looked as she lay dying in the artist's garret, still she sang like a nightingale.

When it was over, Julien, who seemed to know all the musicians in Europe, went backstage and invited them to come to an Army party the following week at the Marchesa's flat. As we walked back through the blacked-out streets, choice bits from the opera were re-enacted by a few musically inclined GI's.

I made it my business to get back from the front the following week in time for that party. Peppino did my hair, and brought me out in the mess hall to dry, so that in between ministrations to my coiffure he could bustle back and forth directing the other Italian servants.

The GI's joined busily in the preparations. They set up a long buffet table in the mess hall, and as they buzzed past the corner where

I sat drying my hair they would remark, "Gosh, it looks good to see a woman drying her hair again. Just like home."

Equipped only with egg powder and other assorted ingredients obtained from the mess, the Italian kitchen squad turned out an astonishing variety of native pastries. They produced various sorts of *dolce*, also *torte* with chocolate cream filling; there were *paste di Mandoli assortite*, and best of all, light, flaky twists of *pasticcetti* dusted with sugar and filled with chocolate. And also, there was Spam.

The Spam was an afterthought. Actually its presence was a bit of an accident, as it was introduced as part of the decorations. The decorative scheme was being arranged by the quietest, gravest member of the organization, a special agent named Bill, born and raised in China, who had gone to Harvard and managed stage effects for the dramatic club. In addition to fluent Mandarin, he spoke six Chinese dialects. One of these was so rare that it was known only to a handful of Chinese coolies in a remote Manchurian village. Bill had learned it when his father served there as an Episcopal missionary. When his family moved out, another missionary moved in, and, curiously enough, this second missionary's son also became an agent for CIC.

While we all knew Bill was a wizard with Chinese, we never knew his talents extended to decorating tables. What Bill did to that buffet was miraculous, with those dishes of Italian pastry, an assortment of pink wineglasses, groupings of pink-striped camellias, and a mountain of fruit heaped with studied casualness. This artistic gift seemed surprising in a missionary's child.

Everyone was ecstatic over the result. But not Bill, the perfectionist. "It needs another touch," he kept saying. "More color. More pink. I've bought up all the camellias I can find."

The quartermaster in his infinite wisdom had the answer for that one. A large platter of Spam provided Special Agent Bill with the color note he needed.

We were anxiously discussing the wine shortage when Norm came in with his arms full of wine bottles. Norm was from Brooklyn, and as the CO's jeep driver he was known as Pappy's "Torpedo Man." "Good job getting this vino in time for the party," said Norm. "Usually I go out in good spirits and come back without any."

When the San Carlo singers arrived, they descended on that buffet

table like a cloud of ravens. Little Pina Esca, the plump soprano, looking like a Koala bear in her fur coat (as usual the place was as chilly as
a meat cooler), led the rush for the mess room and began devouring
Spam. Ponno, the thin tenor, and Ugo, the hawk-faced baritone, tripped
over each other on the way to the Spam platter. An unidentified waxy-
faced lady in lavender and gold lace began consuming Spam as though
each slice would be her last morsel on earth. The orchestra conductor,
little black-haired Mario Pasquariello, headed for that pile of pink-
sliced luncheon meat like a homing pigeon. It would have done the
manufacturers good, whose feelings have been a bit hurt, I understand,
by wisecracking Army references to their product, to see how the entire
San Carlo Opera Company took to Spam.

The preference of the singers suited the Americans right down to the
ground. It gave all of us a chance to eat the unfamiliar and extremely
delicious Neapolitan pastries.

When at last we got those opera singers properly fed we went to the
piano. The Marchesa's ballroom looked particularly festive that night,
because Peppino had written WELCOME in big soap letters, both in English and Italian, all over the mirrors; and in the center of the floor, in
place of the dishpan which customarily stood there to catch the drip,
he had placed a big washtub full of flowers.

The maestro, explosive little Mino Campanino, took his place at the
keyboard. As he accompanied his flock, he conducted them with ges-
tures, with his eyes, with his whole body. Campanino is one of the best
voice coaches in Italy; he is said to know both the words and music of
every opera ever written. We had a new tenor that night, tall Nino
Adami, good-looking in the Hollywood manner, and a rising star in the
San Carlo. He sang duets with the lace-dressed wax lady, Iola Rizzuto.
But the central figure among the singers was always sprightly little Pina
Esca. She begged off singing opera. She wanted to sing American jazz,
so she broke into *Yes, Sir, That's My Baby* in a strange tongue that was
neither Italian nor merely la-la-ing. I think she imagined she was singing English.

Then Captain Swarzwalder sang *Vision Fugitive* from *Hérodiade* by
Massenet. Pina sang *Dancing Cheek to Cheek*. Next John gave a swing
version of *The Sheik of Araby*, while Smitty grabbed Pina and whirled
her off her tiny feet like a jitterbug with a bobby-sock girl. I am sure we
were witnessing the finest swing ever danced by a Mormon missionary

and an opera star. "Pina's really a cutie-pie," was the verdict of Cheech.

Even Pappy and Walt sang. Walt was a former football player and sang like one, while Pappy shifted quaintly from key to key, as usual. They had only one number, *When Irish Eyes Are Smiling*, and ever since one day when they had surprised everyone by hitting high A flat by accident, they broke into *Irish Eyes* whenever they could get anybody to listen.

The only person who was not allowed to sing was poor Smitty. Since he was under training, the maestro had forbidden him to sing until he was "better developed."

It was when John started singing Negro spirituals in that beautiful, steady voice of his that Mino Campanino got really excited. Captain Swarzwalder was to sing at the San Carlo. The maestro would not take no for an answer. So one month later from the stage of the great opera house, the captain sang selections from *The Barber of Seville* to a large cheering audience of GI's.

Smitty had to take a lot of kidding from CIC about his need of being better developed. One night he came home after his singing lesson in a perplexed state of mind. The maestro had directed him to gargle daily with a glassful of wine. This was a problem for the young missionary whose creed of behavior forbade his drinking wine. It was a problem which the rest of CIC were delighted to help him with. For hours they discussed with Smitty how much gargling was possible without letting a few drops of wine trickle down your throat. Throughout the next week, their favorite topic at mess was whether or not it should be counted as a sin if their Mormon swallowed a bit of wine by accident.

All CIC characters were sorry when this interesting problem was solved. Smitty returned from his next singing lesson with the report that because his Italian was none too good he had not understood his teacher's directions very well. The maestro's instructions had been, not to gargle daily with a glassful of wine, but to use daily a wineglassful of gargle.

CHAPTER 11

"See Naples"

THE ORANGE CLUB in Naples opened to a literal baptism of fire. No other night club in the world has ever had a more spectacular opening. Someone like Norman Bel Geddes, working on a colossal scale, might have designed it, but he never would have been able to get the facilities. It had to be an international job.

The Germans floated candelabra flares over the new club; the Americans threw up tinseled curtains of ack-ack around it; and the British navy in the harbor below sent up fountains of fire from each destroyer. There were so many tracers streaming upward from the hills and the water that it looked as if thousands of jugglers had been hired to toss up golden pingpong balls.

It was such a hot opening for the club that most of the guests never got there. The competition was too strong from Al's Place that night. There was a chain of these establishments all over the city, with signs to the entrance marked Al Ricovero (Italian for air-raid shelter), so everybody who got caught on the way to the Orange Club popped into the nearest Al's Place.

Those of us who made it watched the attack from the circular terraces of the modernistic pile of concrete and chromium which the Army had requisitioned for an officers' club. Finally the flak fragments falling from our own guns emplaced above us became too thick for safety and we went inside. There we sat, with equal insecurity, under the immense dome of blacked-out glass over the dance floor, listening to dive bombers zooming overhead, and holding our breath each time a bomb dropped, while the building shook like a giant glass birdcage.

Major Papurt, the CIC CO, sat at a table on the edge of the dance floor. Pappy's sharp, kind eyes through his silver-rimmed spectacles watched everybody. In a place like this, where soldiers come for recreation, it is especially important that no unfriendly listeners who could pick up significant scraps of conversation be hired by mistake.

When the aerial visitors went home (and at least three of them never got the chance to go home—they had fallen like flaming comets into the Bay of Naples), the excellent Army orchestra warmed up, and the few of us there did a little dancing.

We should have taken more advantage of the uncrowded floor that opening night, for from then on dancing in the Orange Club was like trying to dance in the middle of Times Square on New Year's Eve. Overnight the place became the most lively and popular night club on the European continent.

It was difficult to understand how the glass and chromium walls could hold without bursting all the fliers, infantrymen, medicos, artillerymen, WAC's, Red Cross girls, and nurses who crowded in every night. Yet each succeeding night they managed somehow to pack in even more. British Army and Navy officers came with the gray-trousered English and Scottish girls who drove for them. French officers brought members of "La Section Sanitaire Automobile Féminine." I was glad to see these French girls have a chance for recreation, for their small group went through great danger on their jobs. Driving our American Lend-Lease ambulances, and trained to do all their own maintenance and repair work, I had seen them far up in the hills, well within shell range. It was always a surprise to catch that vivid slash of lipstick from the front seat of an ambulance; when you saw it you knew it was a *conductrice sanitaire*.

One day I came back after two particularly discouraging weeks at the front. It had rained so much that several of the Zeiss lenses for my Linhof and, still worse, one of my Rolleiflexes also, had been put completely out of order by dampness getting between the shutter leaves. The batteries for my speed guns had worn down so badly that frequently my flash bulbs refused to go off, and when they did, often I could tell by the delayed sound of the shutter that the equipment was out of synchronization. I had spent every night tinkering with my equipment, and testing out batteries, trying to work with only the freshest of them; but still I knew I had lost many good action pictures. I was particularly distressed at this loss, for I had had the chance to photograph an entire Bailey bridge being erected in six and one half hours' time, and also other interesting operations of the engineers, many of them under shell fire.

Arriving in Naples, the first thing I did was to hunt up Peppino and "vet" him again. Lieutenant Smith saw me come in, and remarked, "Peggy, your halo looks a bit chipped today." Smitty had a mystical way of expressing himself. I suppose being a Latter-Day Saint he knew about things like halos, and whenever I came back happy because I felt my results had been good, Smitty would say, "Peggy, your halo is very bright today."

However, Peppino proceeded to ignore the halo and put my tousled head promptly under the Marchesa's shower. Then he did a sculptural upswept job and topped it off with a couple of pink camellias. Captain Julien had come back to the billet by the time I emerged with this un-warlike coiffure. "Peggy," he exclaimed, "why don't you go to the Orange Club dressed like a girl."

So I hunted around until I found an Italian maid to press my Adrian gown, which until then had remained crushed into a wrinkled ball at the bottom of my barracks bag. Then Julien, Pappy, Laughing Boy, both the Mormons, Walt, and I went to the Orange Club.

We had a little delay getting into the building, at first, because of my civilian clothes. The rule was strict that only Army personnel could attend, and I had to show my war correspondent's credentials before I was admitted.

The best dancers there were always the American nurses. No matter how crowded the floor, some energetic little jitterbug of a nurse was always able to clear a circle around herself, going through her Jersey Bounce or swing steps with a dash that brought cheers from the soldiers. No nurse or WAC or RCA girl, and no woman war correspondent either for that matter, was able to take ten consecutive steps across the floor of the Orange Club without being cut in on. But I always thought there was a certain element of sadness in this; the men outnumbered the girls 100 to one. Some of the men, of course, were stationed in Naples, and had frequent opportunities for normal entertainment, but many of those who flooded the Orange Club came during their few brief days of leave. The chance to hear an American girl's voice—just a word or two—was something they craved. The chance to dance a few steps with a girl was something that reminded them of home. Sometimes the place seemed haunted with that particular brand of loneliness which one finds only in the densest crowds. And I could never forget that many of these boys would go back into the rain and mud and screaming dangers of the hills, never to return.

The Red Cross was doing a busy and able entertainment job in Naples, and in other centers as well, and close behind the front one often ran into their clubmobiles. In Naples one of the chief recreation centers for soldiers was the great Red Cross center, with its enormous movie theater. A new picture was run every day at four in the afternoon, and huge as the place was, you had to arrive half an hour ahead of time to get a seat. Often the Red Cross people would have obscure troubles with the power system and the crowd would sit there for an hour or more impatiently hooting and whistling while the picture flickered on and off, until finally a flustered and pretty Red Cross girl would have to make a speech stating that all efforts to fix up the generator had failed, and there could be no movie until the next day.

One of the main diversions of soldiers on leave in Naples was going on a silk-stocking hunt. Silk hose was getting scarcer and costlier each week. From 120 lire a pair ($1.20), the price when our troops took Naples, they had risen to 650 lire or more. The boys who came in with the first wave were able to send their sweethearts in America gifts of silk stockings as clear as glass, but the rush for these hose had been so great that only brownish streaked ones were left for sale.

It still was possible to buy good gloves. Often if I happened to be walking through Via Chiaia, soldiers would come up to me and bashfully ask me what size glove I wore. Whenever a boy stopped me with a question like this I would take a few minutes to go into a shop with him, and try to help make a decision, based on the nebulous description of that girl back home, as to what size and color gloves would suit her.

Sometimes my advice would be asked on shoes, but this was rarer, for the Italian shoe styles were too extreme in design to attract many GI buyers. I thought them attractive, however, with their exaggerated soles and bright colors. The Italian girls, although seldom well dressed, looked smartly shod as they clattered along on their high little platforms of wood or cork.

The American soldiers soaked up almost anything that appeared for sale. All traces of fine Italian jewelry quickly disappeared, and the showcases lining the shopping streets became as thickly corroded with junk as a ship's hull with barnacles. Many shopwindows were literally encrusted with rank growths of coral—prickly necklaces, spiny bracelets, and uncomfortable ornaments. All the ugly and poorly-cut cameos, the residue of generations of tourist trade, crept out of hiding. You could look into any jewelry display case and see hundreds of identically carved miniature faces scowling in their wall-eyed way at window shoppers.

Even the Isle of Capri became infected with this creeping epidemic of gadgets; but the souvenir peddlers could not destroy its charm. This lovely spot was turned over to the Air Force as a rest center; a staff of Red Cross girls handled recreation facilities. The ancient buggies, with their still more ancient drivers, who had catered to tourists, now drove pilots and bombardiers around the flower-bordered roads and steep, banked terraces. Sometimes nurses and WAC's had time on leave to take the three-hour boat trip to the island, and their popularity with the vacationing fliers was, of course, tremendous.

However, of the myriads of lonely soldiers who flooded into Naples and other rear areas for their brief and well-earned leave, most stayed lonely. I have often thought that the boys who drifted to streetwalkers went there largely for companionship. I remember once seeing a nice-looking, freckled-faced boy—he could hardly have been twenty—walking along the Santa Lucia water front swinging a young Italian girl by the hand. She was barelegged and rather ragged, and her straight black hair hung childishly down to her shoulders. I know nothing about that particular girl, but I could read in the lad's face that what he craved was friendliness. He was desperately lonely and homesick.

Posters warning against "V.D." covered every wall; but these posters could not give adequate warning against a second closely associated danger. Inevitably, by the very nature of the work, many prostitutes were in the pay of enemy agents. Although the glamorous spy of fiction is conspicuously lacking from this war, thousands of more insignificant and more sordid imitations exist. Probably few of them comprehend the role they fill; they are paid to pass on whatever scraps of information they glean, which will be fitted by experts into the total pattern of espionage.

Along the water-front streets there were still a few restaurants operating which had not been bombed out. I don't know where they found the food, for black-market prices had reached astronomical heights. Often the waiters would request regular customers to bring their own bread; and on the rare days when meat was served, the proprietor would impart that knowledge in whispers only to his favorite clients. But if there was no meat, you could always get bowls of tiny shellfish, steam-

Church is any day soldiers can go.

"Many are the Hearts . . ."

Washday for a mechanized army.

Army bread is absolute tops.

Salvage depots like this one save money.

A parts trailer carries everything from a 12-pound sledge to a rat-tailed file.

A bulldozer can pull anything that has two ends. If it hasn't any ends, a 'dozer will push.

Why the Army waited.

"When I get home I'm going to the Automat and play it like a jukebox."

Someone always said, "What I'd like is a big, juicy steak."

The Army requires vast maintenance, from watches to tanks. T/5 Perry Watson (top photo) came to the Fifth Army from Tiffany's.

Mobile water point, first thing the Army puts up when it sits down. The water is pumped out of a river, purified in the canvas tanks, and hauled away by an unending stream of tank trucks.

Big rifles and little rifles—there are more of the little rifles and in the end they win wars, but both need repairs to keep shooting.

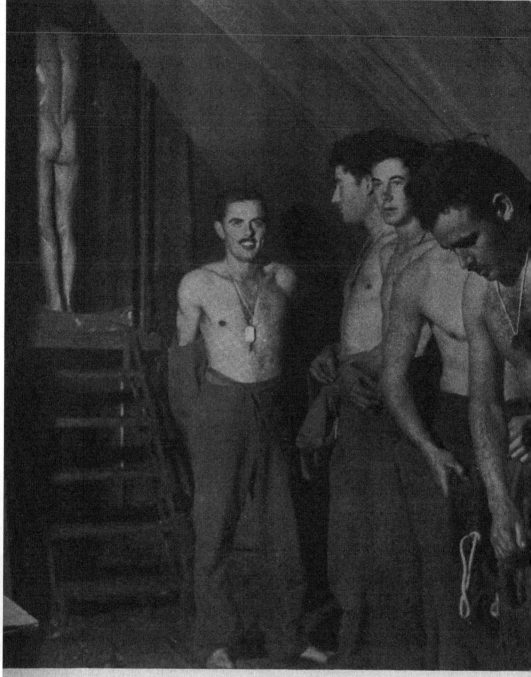

Delousing station.

The Piper Cub pilots made fine quarters out of the crates their planes came in.

Not even the engineers could figure out what the principals in this sculpture were supposed to be doing.

"Dear Mom—I broke the camera!"

On this trip Padgitt and I lived on C rations.

When the German shell hit this antiaircraft truck it was only an incident in a busy day to Corporal Padgitt.

Propaganda is a weapon, too. This shell is being loaded with surrender passes
to fire over the German lines.

These are Fighting Frenchmen.

Nerve ganglion.

ing and delicious. Prices were exorbitant, however, and military personnel were permitted to eat only in establishments which had passed rigorous Army health inspection.

As you ate your shellfish and sipped your vino, you listened to a band of determined violinists and vocalists, the musicians sometimes outnumbering the customers. You had to listen, because they drowned out conversation. Lying in wait outside, flower vendors grimaced through the windows. Once you emerged, several of them would always follow you. The chief item they had for sale was a kind of synthetic camellia tree. Startlingly red-striped and pink-mottled camellias were wired into the shape and size of a blueberry bush. For this highly perishable object, the asking price was two hundred lire, the selling price one hundred.

My favorite restaurant was literally a hole in a wall. It was carved out of the same rocky cliff which housed the great Axis airplane factory that had been left wrecked by the Germans. Two cracked and patched casement windows overlooked the divinely beautiful Naples Harbor, which swept crescent-shaped to the foot of Mt. Vesuvius. In this cave restaurant the steamed clams were tinier and choicer, bread was even scarcer, and the musicians were less noisy. It was not that they were less determined than in other restaurants; they were simply older and feebler. My favorite was a trembling old man who sang *Funiculi, Funicula, Santa Lucia,* and all the Italian standbys through teeth so precariously set in their aged gums that one wondered how they stayed in his skull at all. The song he sang best was *Tell Me That You Love Me Tonight,* for his aged voice seemed to suit the haunting tune.

Once a group of British Tommies sat at the next table; I could tell from their conversation that they had been stationed in the desert and had just been transferred from Africa. One of them spoke to me; we had been torpedoed together at the beginning of the North African invasion and this always creates a bond. We signed each other's Torpedo-Club bills—similar to the Short-Snorter bill of membership for those who have flown an ocean, but this club is eligible only to people who have been torpedoed.

My fellow torpedoee begged me to join his party. "You're the first white woman we've had a chance to talk to for ten months," he explained. Before the evening was over we had consumed a good deal of vino, left platters of empty clamshells, and sung so many English, Scottish, and American songs that we had for once completely drowned out the orchestra with its singing skeleton.

The quartermaster had done a fine job stocking the new Post Exchange which the Army opened in a large building, once a store and still relatively free of bomb damage. You could buy eight packages of cigarettes each week, and allotments of candy and chewing gum; also whatever tooth paste, shaving cream, toothbrushes, and soap you needed. A separate counter was established for women in the service, with face creams, lipsticks, and nail polish. Men were not allowed to patronize this department, but frequently a soldier waylaid a WAC or a nurse, asking her to buy a lipstick or a box of face powder which he could give to some Italian girl.

Nothing made a soldier so unhappy as to have his well-meaning family send him a package of the same things he could buy in the PX. I remember once seeing Laughing Boy open a package with eager anticipation and then exclaim: "I always thought I had such intelligent parents." In the box were four tubes of shaving cream, two of tooth paste, and two toothbrushes.

Welcome gifts are fruitcake, which keeps, the kinds of candies rarely available at the PX such as fine chocolate or peanut brittle, some delicacy which the folks back home know their boy likes particularly (I remember Sergeant Benelli, the deep-sea diver who helped clean up Naples Harbor, kept begging his folks to send him salami). Unwelcome gifts are chewing gum, the small packages of hard candies which soldiers can buy plenty of, and the same brands of canned fruit and meats which he gets in his Army rations. I remember being billeted during the Tunisian campaign in an oasis in the middle of the Sahara where the best dates in the world are grown. When the Christmas packages from home finally arrived, late but welcome, a large number of Air Force boys found that their wives had sent them boxes of Dromedary Dates. The saddest sight in the Army is to see some GI receive a package from home, open it all smiles, and find he is the recipient of the same Spam, politely termed "luncheon meat," which the quartermaster has been feeding him for months, perhaps years. Good gifts are books, magazine subscriptions, in fact, any reading matter. If your boy follows the latest song hits, send him some sheet music; many soldiers are occasionally within reach of a piano in one of the Red Cross centers. If he is a pipe smoker he will be overjoyed with a gift of fine pipes. The best gifts of all are photographs of the people back home, whom he thinks about and misses constantly.

Each time I returned to Naples for a short rest I used to try to get my notes into shape and send a package of film back to the War Department. The system was to have both negatives and notes go back in the Army pouch to the Pentagon Building. The films were developed in Washington, either by the Signal Corps or by *Life* technicians under Army supervision. Only those pictures which passed censorship were sent on to *Life*. Since my mission was partly for the Army Service Forces, those of my pictures which could not be published could still be used by the War Department. Certain technical subjects had to pass British as well as American censors. At the review desk, in the Pentagon Building, the picture censors went over every photograph very fairly and carefully, and often helped us to save a picture for publication where only part of the photograph revealed restricted subjects. In this case they would indicate what portions of the picture must be retouched before publication. Caption material was censored twice. First my rough notes were reviewed: these served only as a basis for *Life*'s writers, who would draw upon them for captions as the layouts were compiled. Then the completed layout was censored once more in Washington, so that text and pictures could be reviewed as a whole before publication.

In order to give my New York office plenty of data to work with—of which only a few lines might appear in print—I sent many closely typed pages of background material. Corporal Padgitt helped me with this, referring to his neat little notebook, in which he had kept the names and home towns of anyone showing prominently in the photographs, matched with numbers on each roll and pack when it was exposed. My most valuable collaborator on caption material was Captain Joe Deutschle, who was a well of useful information about Army affairs.

As the Italian campaign wore on, Naples became softer and more comfortable. Air raids came seldom, although when the Luftwaffe visited they did a thorough job, leaving scars in all the streets bordering the harbor. As the campaign progressed in Italy, a larger number of headquarters offices moved from Africa and Sicily to Naples, and the city became more crowded and gayer with that large proportion of our soldiers who carry on a multitude of behind-the-lines jobs and thus never see the front.

A new "night club" was opened, the Peninsular Base Section Officers'

Club in the Bank of Naples building, for the use of the PBS. The large, formal board-of-directors' room, paneled in dark wood, was requisitioned for a dance hall, and was run by Major Ralph Graeme Smith of Philadelphia. This was an odd change of profession for an insurance broker, but the Army squeezes its men into unfamiliar molds. The ponderous Bank of Naples building always had such an atmosphere of gloom that we referred to the PBS Club as the Mausoleum.

The president of the Bank of Naples, previously a strong Mussolini supporter, was safely in jail. It was said that he had had just enough time to say good-by to the Germans on one side of the city before hastening to the other side to welcome the Americans. He had cut quite a swath with his entertaining in the beginning of the occupation, hoping by his charm and hospitality to ingratiate himself with Allied officers. However, his indelible Fascist connections were proved, and to prison he went. There were many similar efforts on the part of a group of titled Italian Fascists to stay in circulation, buying their way by cocktail parties and dinners. In some quarters this method was fairly successful for a time. Americans as a whole are unsuspecting, politically, and tend to repay hospitality with hospitality. There was a certain naïveté about the attitude of some of our officers toward these invitations from Italian dukes and countesses. Then the Army issued a special directive warning officers to look for political implications in cocktail parties, and as time went on many of the more dubious civilians were interned, or at least had their cars and telephones taken away from them.

The general character of the rear areas grew more comfortable and pleasurable. But, more and more often, one's jeep became blocked by angry crowds who were demonstrating in the streets against some black-market operator. Their anger was directed not so much against the Americans, as against their own food profiteers who still managed to flourish; these markets were partly fed by local Italian farmers; however, these profiteers flourished in no small part because of what American supplies they were able to divert to the black market. The amount of leakage from our Army personnel was, I believe, inconsequential. Some trading was done, of course—I remember going into a small shop once, and hearing a sailor negotiate with the proprietor over a carton of cigarettes which he wished to sell for the current black-market price of

$1.75. "Oh, don't show me another carton of cigarettes!" exclaimed the shopkeeper. "I've got thousands of them."

I was always troubled in the case of AMG with what seemed an intense preoccupation concerning what the public back home might be saying. Of all the officers I knew, these were the only ones who gave even a thought to public opinion back in America. Their job was not an easy one. There was one time when they had only enough flour left for three days, and food riots among civilians were becoming a grave threat. Yet often in the midst of such difficulties AMG spent so much time thinking about whether or not they were getting a bad press that I wondered if they had time to think about their work at all. It seems to me that you can do one of two things: put your mind on your work, or worry about what people are saying about you. The two do not mix.

There was another problem which went even deeper than the food question. In Italy, as on a greater scale in Germany, the effects of Fascism have left their mark on the minds of the people. The only way to leave constructive results behind us in these occupied countries—in fact, the only way to insure future peace in the world—is through education of the young.

In Italy, it seemed to me, we were neglecting a magnificent opportunity. It was not enough to conquer this territory if we did not educate it in such a way that we could live at peace with it in the future. There still were fine minds available at the Italian universities, men who were known for their anti-Fascist ideas. Why not sift out those democratic thinkers who remained, and help the educational system of Italy back on its feet? * Children were roaming the streets, sitting huddled in the caves and tunnels of Naples, growing up to a future of ignorance and prejudice. It mattered little whether the reasons for educating these waifs were humanitarian or based on hardheaded insurance for the future. They were growing up; why not take a hand in raising a future generation that would not bear arms against us, that would understand a democratic way of life?

If this is important in Italy, how much more important it will be when we get into Germany. There an educational job of colossal proportions will face us. It will be difficult, partly because we do not know just what

* I learn that since I left Italy some steps have been taken in the direction of education for Italian children. Textbooks with a democratic slant are now being supplied.

we want to teach, and partly because we have had no practice. Italy could serve as a training ground for the great task that awaits us with Nazi-trained youth.

What is the use of all this bloodshed unless we insure the future for civilization and for peace? What is the use of leaving all these American boys behind on the battlefields, if we leave occupied countries unchanged when we move on? The fault begins not with our armies. The fault begins with us at home.

We are genuinely a freedom-loving people, and freedom is more than a word to us; but the added element of leadership is needed here. If we had a living political philosophy, if democracy were an articulate passion with us, we would be able to communicate it to others. There is no use fighting a war unless we leave behind us a better world, and to do that we must get the youth of Europe on our side.

CHAPTER 12

Salt of the Earth

"IT WON'T hurt much longer, Buddy," Lieutenant Colonel Sanger was saying as he adjusted the tube in the throat of the soldier who lay on the litter. Corporal Padgitt and I paused with the cameras near the operating table. We had come up from Naples to do a series on the work of the Medical Corps, which was one of the many varied activities coming under the Army Service Forces. The Corporal and I stood there watching the gentle and skillful movements of the surgeon, working on a boy who had been drowning in his own blood.

Colonel Sanger glanced up for an instant from his work. "Go right ahead and take pictures if you want to," he said. "It's not a pretty sight, but war is no pink tea party. It's important for people back home to have a chance to see what things over here are really like."

I found it hard at first to take photographs in the face of so much suffering, but with the operating surgeon so absorbed in his work, it became increasingly easier for me to become equally absorbed in mine. I realized that people at home wanted to know what their boys were going through. They had a right to know, and it was my assignment to portray the reality of war as I found it.

The soldier on the operating table had been brought in earlier that morning with a hole in his throat and chest and a wound in his stomach, caused when a shell had smashed into a stony ledge on Mt. Maggiore, flinging fragments behind a rock where he and his companions were snatching a little sleep.

To keep the boy from smothering, Colonel Sanger was siphoning out the blood from the lungs through a metal tracheotomy tube, and the soldier's own blood was being returned to him through intravenous injection. An additional injection needle carried plasma into his system.

The windpipe had been broken and the boy was breathing through the hole in his throat. As I started taking photographs, Colonel Sanger

111

began probing through the same hole to patch up the tear in the boy's chest. At the foot of the litter, a cluster of white-capped, white-gowned surgical assistants incongruously wearing muddy boots leaned over the white-draped patient. They were removing a slug of steel from the small intestines and closing the rent in his abdomen.

"What causes that puffy look in his face?" I asked.

"That's due to the air that kept escaping when his windpipe was broken," the surgeon explained. "The air kept infiltrating under the skin during the whole time he was being transported back to the hospital."

That process of transportation had taken less than five hours. Because of the enormously shortened time which elapses between the time a man is wounded and the time he reaches the operating table many lives which would have been lost in the last war are being saved today. Evacuation and field hospitals are closer to the front than they have ever been before in the history of the American Army.

I noticed that a card, like a baggage check, was attached to the patient's arm and gave the detailed history of his trip to the hospital. It was at 3:15 in the morning that he was picked up by a couple of medical-aid stretcher-bearers who sprinkled sulfa on his wounds. It must have been a slippery trip for them carrying this boy on a litter down the rocky slopes of Mt. Maggiore, but by a quarter after five they made it to the medical-aid station situated in a cross-shaped trench at the foot of the mountain.

There the soldier was given plasma and morphine injections, and continued his bumpy way in a Medical Corps jeep. At 6:30, he was driven to a group of ambulances camouflaged under nets slung among the ruins of a stable. In one of these ambulances he continued his rough trip to the clearing station. At a quarter to seven he was carried into the receiving tent of the evacuation hospital, from there he was taken to the shock tent where he was given more plasma, from there to the X-ray room where photographs were made of his wounds, and from there the patient and the dripping X-ray negatives were carried to the operating tent.

By 8:12 Colonel Sanger had read the story which the still wet pictures had to tell, and begun the delicate task of pumping out the lungs to keep the boy from drowning in the leakage of his own blood.

The patient was moving his lips a little now but making no sound.

Colonel Sanger, realizing that the boy wanted to talk and was finding it impossible because of the air escaping from the broken windpipe, placed his fingers over the hole in the trachea and said, "Try to talk now, Son." We heard the boy murmur feebly, "I'm thirsty." "That's fine, Buddy," said Colonel Sanger. "See, you can speak now."

He took a small sponge and laid it on the boy's lips to moisten them. Because of the stomach wound, I knew they could not give him water. With a look of great tenderness, as though he were teaching something to a child, the Colonel took the soldier's hand and gently placed it over the opening in his throat, thus forcing the air up against the larynx so the boy would be able to speak.

After several feeble tries, he found he could do it himself. It seemed to me that an expression almost of happiness came into the puffy face. The lad felt so much less helpless when he knew he could talk. To learn he could speak after all did a great deal to relieve the growing dread he must have felt before he discovered the extent of his wounds.

The Colonel was so absorbed and so earnest. It meant so much to him each time that boy managed to utter a feeble word. "Will he ever be normal again?" I asked. "Oh, yes, he'll recover all right. He'll be as good as new," said the Colonel.

Lieutenant Colonel Paul W. Sanger is one of the best thoracic surgeons in the Army. He is thirty-seven years old, has a narrow handsome face with precisely chiseled features, and a mind as sharp as his own surgical instruments. Dr. Sanger had been an instructor in surgery at Duke University Hospital for six years and it was during the time he was practicing in Charlotte, N. C., that the war broke out.

He was sharing an office with a brain surgeon, Dr. William R. Pitts, and he and Pitts, together with other surgeons from Charlotte, decided to volunteer as a unit for service in the American armed forces. It happened that General George Marshall was passing through Charlotte and Dr. Sanger broached the subject. It was with the blessing of General Marshall that the surgeons from Charlotte gathered up medical men and nurses from both the Carolinas and near-by regions. This group later became incorporated into the 38th Evacuation Hospital.

When they pitched their hundred tents and set up their 750 beds close behind Mignano, near the ridge of hills bordering Cassino Valley, the hospital had a staff of approximately three hundred. Since the officers, both nurses and doctors, were Southerners, and most of the enlisted personnel came from Pennsylvania and New York State, some wag put up a sign reading "Mason & Dixon Line" between the nurses' and enlisted men's tent areas.

The "38th Evac" had been in the field since D Day plus one in Africa, they had followed our Army through Sicily, and by the time I saw them in Italy they had become experts at adapting themselves to the most rigorous conditions. They had carried their own water pipes, their own water-storage tank, and their generator for light and power through these many months of war. Later, when they were to move on to Anzio, they picked up and relaid these pipes once more.

The surgeons had learned how to pitch their tents to suit the lay of the land each time they met a new set of field conditions. Their orthopedic surgeon, Captain Robert Augustine—who had worked from the tropics to the Arctic, in South America and in Alaska—plotted out each new hospital area so that patients could travel in a continuous line from receiving tent through shock ward, through X-ray into the operating tent at the front end and out the back tent flaps into a convalescent ward.

The nurses had learned to build small dams and mudbanks to keep their tent floors from flooding in the rain. They knew how to tighten their tent pegs to keep their shelters from sailing away in windstorms, and how to loosen their tent ropes again when the tentage dried out in the sun and shrank.

They had raised the process of bathing in a helmet to a high science. The helmet rests on an empty ration can so that it doesn't start tipping over when you get the water nice and soapy. You keep on your galoshes until you get down to the feet. Your tentmate helps you scrub your back.

The nurses gather up extra comforts for tent furnishings as they travel. Those I saw ranged from straw rugs which the girls purchased from the Arabs in Tunis to a gilt-edged, full-length mirror which they salvaged from a bombed palace they passed on their journey forward through Italy.

When I encountered the unit at their location by the side of Highway Six, First Lieutenant Hallie Almond was in charge of the sixty nurses. Pale eyes and pale hair gave her a look of fragility in sharp contrast to the rugged life for which she had volunteered. I saw Lieutenant Almond first when she was pushing her way out of a tent, carrying several pair of mud-caked galoshes.

"I thought the girls might feel better if I washed off their boots for them. They have been crying."

"Why are they crying?" I asked.

"I wish I knew," she said. "They never answer me when I ask. It's a fatigue neurosis. They just can't help it, living in the mud and taking the same thing every day; but I have noticed that they only cry when the work is lightest. The minute we get a flow of badly wounded patients, they are back on their feet, smiling and telling little jokes to make the boys feel better. I'm trying to arrange some trips for them so that they can go to Naples to see the sights. Maybe some of them can get to Capri once in a while, or at least get to a dance or a movie now and then."

Naples was only two hours' drive away, and the Orange Club was its Mecca. I was always delighted when I recognized girls I had photographed leaning over hospital tables and tending desperately wounded soldiers, laughing and dancing like any bunch of nice American girls off for a good time. Such a transformation! It was hard to believe these were the same girls, jitterbugging around the crowded dance floor. It meant just as much to the nurses as to the soldiers to have this brief holiday from war.

These nurses surely earned the rare dances and movies. During the heaviest day of battle casualties, their hospital received 238 cases. It was a light day that produced as few as seventy. Often it was regular procedure for the nurses, doctors, and technicians to work the clock around with the nine operating tables occupied at all times.

The difficulties of the Medical Corps were increased many times by the Italian mud. The mud did much more than merely make matters inconvenient for them. It greatly increased the hazards of infection.

When our soldiers left North Africa for Italy, they met a new hazard, the danger of gas gangrene. The soil of Africa had been little touched by agriculture; but in Italy, the earth for generations had been fertilized with animal and human waste. Thus any foreign matter in a wound could give rise to the most serious infection.

To check this, drastic measures often had to be taken, such as the swift amputation of an arm or a leg. Surgeons were frequently faced with what is always a dreadful decision—to take the chance and treat a mangled leg, or to amputate. "In a gas-gangrene case, they are dead or on the mend within twenty-four hours," one of the surgeons told me.

Antitetanus injections, given when the boys were picked up on the field, helped to combat the danger of infection.

Sulfa has proved invaluable. One of the first things the litter-bearer does when he picks up a wounded soldier on the battlefield is to scatter sulfa powder on the wounds. The soldiers themselves are issued both the powder and sulfa pills; many a wounded man has saved his own life when help was delayed in getting to him.

I was discussing this with Colonel Sanger and I was amazed to hear him say, "The boys, of course, are supposed to take sulfa pills by mouth as soon as they're wounded, but often they don't have any with them."

"Why don't they have them?" I asked.

"Because frequently they have already taken them surreptitiously," the Colonel replied.

"What do you mean, surreptitiously?" I inquired.

"The boys discovered very early in the war that it was a good idea to take their sulfa pills when they were afraid of gonorrhea, so they often get caught on the battlefield without them.

"Between sulfa and plasma," Colonel Sanger continued, "this is a very different war from the last one. Let me show you a case that has just come into the shock tent. We're fighting to keep him alive with plasma."

On a litter propped up on wooden sawhorses under the slanting tent walls was a soldier with a shattered pelvis. He was surrounded by nurses and ward boys who were inserting an injection needle connected by a rubber tube to the amber-colored plasma bottle suspended above the patient's head. His face was cold and clammy and so pale that all blood seemed to have been drained from him. This was almost literally the case.

"He has lost so much blood," said Colonel Sanger, "that even his wounds have stopped bleeding. It's what we call peripheral circulatory failure. There actually is not enough blood left to circulate through his veins and arteries. He is in a state of acute shock. This is a very close case; but he may live, and if he does, he will have plasma to thank for saving his life."

We went on into one of the convalescent wards and stopped by the side of a patient who was recuperating from ten hours on the operating table, during which he had been given six units of plasma and six units of whole blood. To feed him, Nurse Deborah De Shaw of Brooklyn was injecting a glucose solution into his veins. This soldier had received numerous intestinal wounds from the penetration of shell fragments from an air burst.

When the healing process was completed, he would have a few inches less of the amount of equipment which is allotted to the average human being, but he would heal and probably function quite normally for the rest of his life. In the meantime, his convalescence was painful.

He was still delirious. "Stop, that's enough," he kept telling the nurse, trying to shake himself free from the injection needle which was feeding him with glucose. She held his arm still and supported the needle steady. "That hurts," he murmured.

It touched my heart to see this soldier in such pain. I found it very hard to maintain a professional cameraman's attitude, but I tried to keep on working as well as I could. His discomfort would not last much longer, the doctors told me, as the healing was progressing satisfactorily.

The whole process seemed miraculous to me. The surgeons had performed an unusual operation on the boy and were justly proud of the results. Major Pat Imes of Louisville, Kentucky, stopped by and spoke to me in the midst of my work, repeating what Colonel Sanger had already said to me.

"I'm glad you're photographing some of these cases," he said. "They won't look very pretty to the folks back home, but we feel that there has been too much sugar-coating of this hospital business. We think the people back in the States should realize what their boys are going through." Colonel Sanger heartily endorsed the importance of carrying back a true picture of the realities of war, and we tiptoed out of the ward to another tent where he could show me some more cases.

He led me next to a boy who had lost half his upper lip. "He'll be all right, too," said Colonel Sanger. "That boy has a better chance than a lot of cases that come in. You see, we're born with more mouth than we really need. He has enough lip tissue left to do a good patchwork job."

We passed another patient at the end of the convalescent ward who was recuperating from leg and arm fractures. "He ate twelve pancakes when they brought him in two days ago," said Colonel Sanger. "He was the hungriest patient we ever had. All he said when we put him on the operating table was, 'I got the no-food cramps.'

"It's amazing how much good even a hot drink does when they are carried in here wondering if they are going to die. Simply washing his face does a lot for a lad when he is feeling pretty low. Then he sees a woman and knows that war can't be so bad if there are women nurses there. A little of that 'Eve' stuff does a lot of good for those boys when they are brought in from the front."

Padgitt picked up the photographic gear and we pushed our way out under the tent flaps and heard the chaplain starting up his victrola. Making our way through the mud, we passed a small grim pile of amputated legs which a ward attendant was covering with a piece of canvas. As we hurried on, the chaplain's music still reached us clearly. He was playing *Ah, Sweet Mystery of Life.*

Inside the operating tent, I found Major Pitts stooped over a soldier so completely covered with surgical drapes that nothing but a section of skull was visible. He had been given local anesthesia. Major Pitts was probing through a small hole into the soldier's brain.

As I worked, taking progress photographs, I watched the Major draw out thirteen splinters of bone that a shell blast had driven into the brain. The largest fragment was one inch long and half an inch wide. When he finally drew out the last and deepest piece, which lay two inches beneath the surface of the brain, exactly one hour had passed.

"Can he possibly live through all that?" I questioned.

"He has about a fifty-fifty chance," said the Major, "but he may be paralyzed." The soldier's right foot had been completely blown off, but the leg operation had to wait until the more essential work on the brain was completed. As always in the serious cases, an amber-colored plasma bottle hung above the operating table, and plasma was flowing through a rubber tube into his veins, to ward off shock.

After Major Pitts had worked to coagulate the blood, by means of an electric current, he was ready to repair the covering of the brain. To do this, he borrowed a piece of the temporal muscle from the side of the boy's own head, and the wound was closed.

I was astonished the next day to find that the brain patient was able to carry on a normal conversation with me. "How do you feel?" I asked.

"I feel better than I did the time I had my tooth knocked out playing baseball," he said. He smiled a one-sided smile at the Major and me. "That was the time I got my gold tooth," he added.

I questioned him about the type of work he had done before he entered the Army. Ironically, he had worked in a TNT plant.

"I bet you didn't know you were having your picture taken," I said.

"Yes, I did," he said. "I could tell that someone was flashing lights in my face." It seemed a little late to apologize for disturbing someone having his brain operated on, but needless to say, I did apologize—and very humbly, too. I had had no idea he was aware of what was going on around him.

Major Pitts was delighted with the progress the soldier was making and assured me that his recovery would be almost complete, that probably the only remaining trace of the paralysis would be a slightly crooked smile.

The next day I happened to be working up at the front lines, forward of the evacuation hospital. It had been a rough day with shells whooshing into the hillsides and whistling over the roads. When I returned to the hospital to spend the night, I was greeted with, "We expected to see you about now, but we thought they would be bringing you in on a stretcher."

"What made you think so?" I asked.

"They brought in another war correspondent a few hours ago."

I was led to the bedside of Richard Tregaskis, author of *Guadalcanal Diary*. He had been brought in with a skull wound which was almost identical to the one I had photographed, and he had been operated on by the same surgeon.

The skillful Major Pitts had drawn eight bone splinters out of the journalist's brain, and Tregaskis was doing very well indeed, but he doubtless owed his life to the speed with which he had been brought to the operating table. It was less than five hours after he had been wounded, while storming a mountaintop with the Rangers, until he was brought into the receiving ward of the hospital.

"I suppose you don't have to be six foot six to reach up and stop a shell," I told him, "but probably it helps."

"The thing that helped him the most," said Major Pitts, "is the fact that he has a scalp like a bulldog—all corrugated. It made a sweet closing, sort of fell together."

It was less than two months later that Tregaskis and I both left from the same North African airport. We were flying back to the United States. He had made a remarkable recovery and was wearing only a small bandage, about two inches across. "They're going to give me a nice silver plate to wear when I get home," he said. "Maybe you'll autograph it for me."

"What would be the use?" I replied. "Who is tall enough to read anything written on the top of your head?"

Among a group of battle-hardy correspondents, Dick was one of the bravest I knew. Newspapermen are not compelled to go storming mountaintops with Rangers. With Tregaskis, that inner desire to do truly firsthand reporting burned deep and clear.

Richard Tregaskis was one of the many patients who were evacuated by air. Many were moved in hospital ships.

The last thirty miles the patient traveled in Italy, before being transported away from the war zone by sea or air, was made in a hospital train. This was no ordinary train. There were many difficult problems for our engineers to conquer before that train could be set in motion.

First the entire length of track was repaired. Having seen from the air how every tie had been systematically cracked in two, I was able to understand the size of this job. In addition, every rail had been conscientiously broken by means of baby bombs the size of tomato cans placed at thirty-foot intervals.

Next—in all parts of southern Italy—first-, second-, and third-class coaches were gathered in from where they lay among the railroad wreckage the Germans had left behind them. The insides of the cars were stripped, and bunks for patients were built in. Leaky roofs were mended, broken wheels replaced, and shattered windows reglazed.

The reglazing presented difficulties. The engineers had lifted out unbroken panes of window glass wherever they were fortunate enough to find them in bombed buildings and houses, but they had no glass cutters to reduce the windowpanes to proper size. The problem was solved by going to local jewelers and borrowing diamonds with which to cut out new windows for the train.

The hospital train carried 350 patients a day and had a staff of six nurses, four doctors, four cooks, and twenty-nine enlisted men. It started from the Naples railroad yards every morning, gathered a load of wounded by noon, and by midafternoon it had brought them back to Naples, where they were either loaded on planes, swung up in their litters to a hospital ship, or carried to one of the large base hospitals for further recuperation.

The nurses, along with the hospital train staff, had their living quarters right on the train.

The train was actually a hospital on wheels, equipped to handle any medical emergency. The patients traveled in three decks of bunks graduated according to the severity of their wounds, with the most serious cases at the bottom.

It was a welcome sight to the boys to see a flock of pretty Red Cross girls come through the train, passing out candy, cigarettes, and copies of *The Stars and Stripes*. More than one GI was heard to say, "How long has this been going on?" En route they were given hot mess, but their greatest thrill was the discovery that for the first time in many months they found themselves between clean white sheets.

After traveling with the wounded on the hospital train, and recording their journey as far as the deck of the hospital ship which would carry them home, the Corporal and I started frontward again to photograph one of the small, compact field hospitals located directly behind the fighting lines.

During all this work with the wounded, Padgitt had been even more uncommunicative than usual. I thought I knew why. For I found myself deeply moved by what I had seen, by the care our Army takes of its soldiers, and by the immensity of the sacrifices made by so many of our fighting men. As citizens of America, I thought, the many of us who are not called upon to fight must be deserving of this contribution which has been made for us.

The Corporal evidently was thinking along the same lines because unexpectedly he volunteered: "If there's anybody back in America that don't realize what these guys are going through, well, all I say is they should go to the back door to cash their pay checks."

We drove on in silence for several miles, and then he went on, "Those boys we saw that lost a leg or an arm, you don't hear none of them complaining. I suppose they know how near they came to losing their lives. That's all part of the old war game and is to be expected.

"What gets me is there's plenty of us guys that get three hot meals every day, and happen to do a lot of our duties way back out of shell range. Us guys will go home as heroes. Plenty of those guys up front who do go home will go home as 'just another cripple.'"

Ahead of us, marking a muddy lane leading off from the right side of the highway, was a sign: 11TH. FIELD HOSP. RECEIVING. Padgitt swung the jeep into it, trying to avoid ruts cut as sharp as canyons, and as he cautiously piloted the jeep forward, he remarked, "That's one reason I'm glad to get the chance to work up forward with you, Peggy. You can't fool the public in pictures. And people should be shown just what those boys do to become a cripple."

CHAPTER 13

Fifth Army Field Hospital

NURSE BETTY COOK was applying a coat of polish to her nails as carefully as though she were going to a party. Actually she was about to keep a date with a semiconscious boy who had a spray of shrapnel in his chest and face and had lost his left foot. She made an incongruous but pretty picture sitting on her bunk in her striped seersucker hospital dress and high muddy boots, her gentle oval face framed by soft dark hair.

"It's so nice to have a little scented soap and a bottle of nail polish out here," she said. "Yesterday when I was working with the Major, preparing for that traumatic amputation case, I was afraid he was going to scold me about my nails, but he only said, 'It looks good to see a woman with red-painted fingernails again.'"

Cordelia Elizabeth Cook, twenty-four-year-old Kentuckian, was one of ten surgical nurses in the 11th Field Hospital. These girls were working closer to the battle line than American women had ever worked before in this or any other war. Our troops, at this time, were fighting their way through the lowlands of Cassino corridor, and these ten nurses were stationed actually ahead of our own heavy guns. A short stroll in the wrong direction would bring one right into German territory.

This advanced position of the field hospital made it possible to save many of those desperately serious cases inevitably lost in the last war. Here the worst brain, chest, and abdominal cases, which could not stand the long trip to the rear, were taken off the ambulances and given immediate definitive surgery. The evening I arrived with Padgitt, two soldiers had been brought to the hospital within the same hour they were wounded. When strong enough, the patients would be moved back another five miles to the larger evacuation hospital.

The field hospital, marked with its red-painted crosses, was itself laid out in the form of a large cross whose arms were formed of big, continuous wall tents. A wounded soldier entering through the receiving ward could run the whole gamut of treatment without being carried out-of-doors. Near this central cross of canvas were the mess tent and clusters of smaller tents used as the staff's living quarters.

Towering above this small encampment on a mountain peak six miles away was a German observation post. From this height the Germans could survey a fifteen-mile length of Highway Six. If they turned their binoculars southeastward they looked down right into our little tent cluster; northwestward they overlooked Purple Heart Valley.

Whenever the girls had time to glance toward Jerry's mountaintop, they could watch columns of smoke rising from our shell hits, where we were attempting to blast the enemy out of his stubbornly held vantage point. The nurses were learning to ignore the deafening staccato of our guns during the day, but they could never grow accustomed to the way their beds trembled all through the night. Ours and the enemy's artillery crashed back and forth at each other, the two-way traffic of shells passing directly overhead.

Bedtime for the day staff came early in the blacked-out field hospital. I had arrived with Corporal Padgitt at dusk, which, during those winter months, came at five-thirty. The Corporal had gone off to find quarters in the enlisted men's area, and I went to a tent with five of the nurses, where I was to spend the night. It was only seven when blonde little Lieutenant Frances Mosher, of South Bend, Indiana, a coat thrown over her pajamas, stoked up the primitive little wood stove in the center of the muddy floor and heated bath water in an empty apple-butter can. Lieutenant Elsie Nichols began bathing in her helmet, finishing off her feet methodically with foot powder.

Nicky was from Melrose, Massachusetts, a good-natured girl, a bit on the plump side. "One of the first things you learn on this job," she explained to me, "is that even if you don't have time for anything else, you have to take care of your feet."

Tall, slender Lieutenant Ruth Hindman, her blonde hair glistening with rain, burst through the tent flaps. "The whole Volturno is running through our powder room," she said. "We'll have to get out our shovels and deepen that irrigation ditch in the morning."

"That little floating tent you call a powder room is the most forlorn bit of architecture I've ever seen," I commented.

"Oh, it's so much nicer than the slit trench we used to have," replied Ruthie.

Ruthie Hindman was from Johnstown, Pennsylvania, and was one of those generous women who are always cooking something for somebody. She started making cocoa in a plasma can—not mixing cocoa with plasma, to be sure; but in a hospital there are a thousand uses for cast-off plasma cans. The cocoa had just come to a boil when there was a sound like a rising wind rushing out of the mountain toward us.

"Is that theirs or ours?" cried Nicky.

"Theirs," shouted Ruthie.

And instantly all that remained visible of the nurses were four pairs of legs sticking out from under the cots. By the time I had followed their example the sound had reached tornado proportions, when it suddenly came to an end in an abrupt thud.

"That's the first time they've ever aimed at the hospital," exclaimed Nicky, as the girls pulled themselves to their feet.

"Don't worry, honey, that was just a stray one," said Ruthie. "They're not after us; they're trying to knock out those guns beyond us. They aren't going to keep it up."

"There it comes again," shouted Fran, and we fell flat on our faces while a new sound carved a screaming path toward us until all sounds were lost in the deafening roar. It seemed as though the earth would never stop pelting against the tent walls, but at last it was over and we crawled to our feet. The lights had gone, but finally one of the girls found a flashlight and when she switched it on I remember noticing that three C-ration cans had blown through the door of the tent and wedged between a couple of my camera cases.

Then I heard a voice from outside, "You all right, Peggy?" It was Padgitt, and with his help I gathered up some camera equipment and we started out into the darkness. Thirty feet from the tent we were stopped by a tangle of waist-high wires. This was why the lights had gone: the camp's improvised electrical circuit had been strung through the mess tent, adjoining the nurses' quarters.

The Corporal put on his flash, carefully dimming its beam with his hands, and we found that there was no more mess tent. We were standing on the brink of a neat, round shell hole, and strewn about were cans of rations, onions, benches, stoves flung in all directions, and slashed lengths of tent canvas. The CO, Major Bonham, was poking around the ruins, deeply relieved to find that no one was caught under the debris. Three of the hospital staff had been wounded by shrapnel, he told me.

It seemed a miracle that no one had been killed, with the shell falling within less than fifteen yards of the operating tent. The mess sergeant had just stepped out of the tent flaps to get gasoline for his cookstove, and had been blown five yards off his feet. He landed on his face very much surprised, but not at all hurt. Ten minutes later the night staff of thirty-two would have been in the mess tent for coffee and pancakes.

Stumbling over wreckage to the hospital tent, Padgitt and I found the shock ward a gloomy cavern with no electric light. Over each litter hung a small knot of medics in muddy boots, and wearing helmets, diagnosing wounds with only the illumination furnished by their GI flashlights.

The largest group were leaning over a soldier whose thighs had been practically amputated by a high explosive shell. Only raw strips of flesh and skin held the legs to the mangled body, and his right forearm had compound fractures of both bones. The boy's lacerated face was only partially visible under the oxygen mask; from twin bottles, mounted on a standard over his litter, both plasma and whole blood flowed into his veins.

The clay-colored lips, ringed by the oxygen mask, started moving, and Nurse Wilma Barnes leaned over to listen.

"They're taking my blood," whispered the soldier.

"No, Clarence, they're not taking your blood," she said, "they're giving you something to make you stronger."

"Do you learn all their first names?" I asked.

"Always when they come from Texas," replied Wilma Barnes, who was a handsome, black-haired girl from Abilene. "The doctors just automatically call me every time they get a patient from Texas. It makes the boys pep up to know somebody from their home state is taking care of them."

It happened that the greater number of boys being brought in that night were from Texas, since the fiercest of the fighting at that time, on the outskirts of Cassino, was being carried on by the famous 36th Division, largely composed of Texans.

We had thought that first salvo of shells was an accident, but it was only the first of many that screamed over our hospital all through the night. Sometimes every few minutes, and often every few seconds, a warning whistle would sound overhead, and the entire hospital staff—accompanied by the Corporal and myself—would fall flat to the ground.

But as soon as that shell landed, the surgeons, nurses, and ward attendants would rise instantly to their feet and continue their work of taking care of the wounded. There was so much changing and disinfecting of rubber gloves, so much sterilizing of instruments, that a vacant cot next to Clarence's litter filled up completely with gear.

Clarence had lost so much blood that the doctors were giving him whole blood and plasma in both wrists instead of one. They were fighting hard to sustain him through his state of acute shock, until he had rallied enough to be operated on.

The chief surgeon was applying a wire tourniquet around his torn thighs when a whooshlike sound swept over, closer than the rest. "Cross your fingers that it holds," he said as we all hit the dirt.

We had just regained our feet when a particularly loud scream came piercing toward us and we all fell flat. I noticed that Wilma, before she dropped down, took time to check the position of the blood and plasma needles in the boy's wrists. I heard her say, "Hold your arm still, Clarence," and she lay down on the ground beside his cot.

The instant we heard the bang of the exploding shell, Wilma was the first person back on her feet, making sure those transfusion needles had not been jarred out of place.

I remember thinking that it was a privilege to be with people like that.

As we all got off the muddy ground again, one of the surgeons commented, "Just a wee bit different from pounding the marble floors of a big hospital."

"Buy me a one-way ticket to New York," remarked one of the ward boys.

Occasionally a naked electric bulb hanging in the center of the tent blazed on as soldiers working in the ruins managed to make a temporary contact. But always before long the electricity failed again, and the surgeons went back to their flashlights.

A small and terrified dog came crawling in under the tent canvas. "Will somebody put Sad Sack out?" ordered Wilma.

The hours crawled on in their grotesque routine. The periodic whoosh overhead; the dive for the floor; up again and on with the work; the constant changing of blood and plasma bottles. Clarence was on his seventh unit of plasma, and 5000 cc.'s of whole blood had flowed into his veins, a record amount for that hospital.

So much blood was being used that night that the supply was running low. Members of the hospital staff began volunteering to give their blood. Then the truck drivers were called in from out-of-doors; they came, a few silent figures at a time, lying down on any available litter to give their pints of blood, and hurrying out again to work. At last the need of blood became so great that the gun crews from the artillery positions up the road came down in rotation, long enough to donate blood and then go back to their job of shelling the German mountain.

Once more Clarence moved his pasty-colored lips and Wilma leaned down to listen. "No, Son," she said in her soft Texas drawl, "you can't have a cigarette yet. Wait just a little while longer."

The little redheaded Commanding Officer, Major Bonham—"Bon for good in the French language and ham, good in any language," he had told me earlier—came up rolling a replacement oxygen tank. "Things are at their worst," he confided, while shifting the tank. "We're almost out of Type A blood. We're running out of blood citrates which we need for all these transfusions, and now the oxygen is giving out."

He checked the dials. "It's not working properly," he said. "There's only one tank left and that's being used in the operating room. We must keep that patient breathing. We'll have to move Clarence in there."

Clarence was without oxygen for four and one-half minutes while the little procession, headed by Major Bonham carrying the twin bottles on their standards, moved through connecting tents into the white-draped operating tent, where Clarence could again be connected with blood, plasma, and oxygen supply. He shared his new oxygen pressure tank with the patient on the operating table, a boy who had been brought in with multiple wounds of face and chest, and with one third of his thigh shot away.

While Clarence was being moved, Padgitt helped me transfer the camera into the operating ward. When he had me installed in the new location he said, "Can you get along without me for half an hour, Peggy?"

"Of course," I replied, but I was secretly a bit surprised, because never before had the Corporal left me during an emergency.

At the end of half an hour Padgitt came back, looking a little pale. It was only later that I found he had given a pint of his blood—his was Type A, the kind they were short of.

Clarence's breathing had grown so shallow by this time that the balloon at the base of his mask, which should inflate with each breath, lay almost flat on his chest. Captain Floyd Taylor (burly, able surgeon from Haskel, Texas, who helped rescue *Time* magazine's Jack Belden on Salerno beach) began pinching the nostrils under the mask and holding his hands over the mouth, trying to force Clarence to breath deeper.

"He's getting everything for shock that the books have to offer," said Captain Taylor.

Meanwhile Wilma had recognized another Texan on the next table. "How do you feel, Chester?" she inquired.

"Not so good," Chester managed to reply.

The group of helmeted surgeons were now leaning over Chester, debating whether to amputate or try to save his wounded leg, thereby running the risk of gas gangrene. Having decided to try to save Chester's leg, they tied on gauze masks and, still wearing their helmets, began to operate.

It was two in the morning before Chester was moved to the adjoining ward. Meanwhile Clarence had received a total of 6000 cc.'s of blood. He was moving his lips again in their rubber frame, and Captain Taylor tried to catch the words.

"He's asking for watermelon," the Captain explained. "They often ask for their favorite foods when they're near death." Leaning over Clarence, he said, "They're not in season, Son."

"Cover up my feet," Clarence murmured. And then, whispering, "I'm so cold," he died.

I took a last picture of those feet, still in their muddy boots, and with the boy's own rifle strapped between them where it served as a splint for the crushed legs.

The corps men lifted the bloodstained gun away. "Be careful," one of them said, "it may be loaded."

Kindly Captain Taylor bade me good night. "The lad wouldn't have had much left to do with if he had lived," he said, "with both legs and one arm gone."

Wilma and I stumbled home together. Watching death so close before my eyes, I had forgotten the wholesale screaming death being hurled from the mountaintop. The enemy's mountain hung above us silhouetted as though against heat lightning. An occasional brilliant flash threw shadows like those from moonlight across our path.

Back in our tent we found Ruthie, Nicky, and Fran drinking more cocoa. "We just came from Betty's tent," said the girls. "An hour ago she was hit in the elbow by shrapnel, but she had her heavy coat on and the wound isn't serious."

It seemed blessedly normal to be back in the tent chatting with the girls. They were discussing how surprised German prisoners acted to see American nurses so close to the front, and how a captured German officer had said that German nurses do not work within a hundred miles of the lines.*

"It seems to do our boys good to hear a woman's voice," said Ruthie. "When Clarence was brought in today, he said, 'Tell that woman to come over here so we can look at her.' "

"Clarence died," Wilma reported.

"I always get a funny feeling," said Ruthie, "when I have to go through their pockets afterward and take out all the things. So many things they think they've got to have."

"What things?" I asked.

"Always a picture of their girl. That's the first and last thing they'll ask to look at."

I had just voiced a comment on how quiet it had become when the word "quiet" was drowned out by a sound as though the whole German mountain was rushing toward us, and we were back under our bunks again waiting for the sweeping terror to spend itself and die.

"I'm going to make my bed right under my cot," said Nicky, dragging all her bedding to the floor and covering her face with her helmet.

A series of short booms and coughs began echoing through the mountains. "Theirs or ours?" asked Nicky.

"Ours," said Frances. "When you hear the whizz first and the thump afterwards, it's theirs; and when you hear the thump first and the echo afterwards, it's ours."

Whizzes, echoes, and thumps began to intermingle so vigorously that our cots rocked. "Are you going to get under the bed?" Nicky called.

"I'm already under it," Ruthie answered.

It wasn't much longer before we had all dragged our blankets down in the mud and all of us stayed under our beds.

"I pity those poor boys up there," said Fran. "Look at us. We've got

* After the opening of the Normandy beachhead, German nurses were found near the front lines.

heat. And all the comforts. Those poor boys in the foxholes can't even put on a pair of dry socks. They can't even build a fire."

Then the noise of the guns drowned out the conversation again. In the next lull Ruthie spoke up. "I got a letter today that burned me up; 'I hope you can send me some fine laces from one of those picturesque Italian towns.' Lord, when we get to those towns there's nothing left of them."

"I get letters saying 'Send me some souvenirs; I'll pay for them,'" said Fran. "The only souvenirs we can send are pieces of shrapnel."

I had been searching around during this temporary quiet spell for a safer place to put my cameras. Next to my bunk was a small table crowded underneath with barracks bags. I pushed away the barracks bags and placed my cameras there. Then it occurred to me that the spot I had picked for my cameras would be a good place for me. I had just shoved the cameras out and slid under the table with all my blankets when Jerry started in again.

"I'm really scared," said Nicky.

"Come over and get in bed with me," said Wilma. "Then if we die, we'll die together."

A new sound was growing out of the mountain now. It was like a giant stalking toward us over the hills. Closer and closer the giant feet came until the last three steps crashed around us with the loudest sound I had ever heard.

"It's a creeping barrage," said Ruthie.

"I'm worried about those poor boys in the hospital who are still in shock," said Wilma. "It's so much worse for them, because they can't understand how, if they're really in a hospital, it sounds as though they're still in the field."

"Can they tell?" I asked.

"Oh, yes. They lie there and call out the names of the guns."

The giant feet were marching toward us again, and when the last crash had died away Nicky commented, "It's worse than when they bombed our ship in Salerno Harbor."

"It seems as bad as when our ship caught on fire and those poor British nurses got burned to death and we had to leave in lifeboats," said Nicky.

A throaty reverberation began knocking through the hills. "Theirs or ours?" I asked.

"That's thunder," said the girls. It seemed such a benign sound, and, when the rain started pelting on our tent, I decided that the guns would have to stop. But the gun crews in the mountain had decided otherwise, and the pounding rain only made it more difficult for us to distinguish between their guns and ours.

We didn't know until the next morning that shortly after the beginning of the thunderstorm, two boys were killed across the road.

Hairlines of vivid light flashed under the tent flaps and all the pinholes in the canvas began winking on and off. It was as though a brilliant torch flickered on and off through a sieve, each flash a burst from the muzzles of our own guns. Our 105's and 155's were booming repeatedly, and the deeper voice of the 240's was roaring out toward the German-held mountain peak.

"You know what I always think of," said Wilma, "every time they bring a boy in? My kid brother—especially if the soldier's about the same age. Doesn't it always remind you of your brother?"

And the girls began worrying about their brothers scattered throughout the various war theaters of the world. I wondered how these brothers would feel if they could see their brave sisters pancaked under their cots while a two-way barrage passed over their heads.

It was just grim waiting the rest of the night until all the crash and booming faded into tangled echoes beating through the hills. But all nights have to end, and finally we staggered stiffly out into a welcome rainy dawn.*

* Before the reader starts hunting for the photographs of Clarence and Chester, of Betty Cook and Wilma Barnes, and the other nurses described in this chapter, as well as the ambulance drivers and the exploding ammo dump described in the next, I must explain that due to the hazards of war, this entire group of films was lost in transit from Italy to Washington.

CHAPTER 14

We Move Toward the Front

IN THE morning, all over camp, people began digging trenches in their tents right beside their cots, so that the next time the hospital was shelled they could roll right out of bed into their foxholes. Nicky launched on a particularly ambitious excavation, designed to hold her whole cot and her barracks bag.

We had a stand-up breakfast, handed out from the rear end of a truck which had been rushed up with rations. The hospital's food stocks had been completely blown to pieces—although many of us picked up edible odds and ends that had been blasted into our tents. The truck had brought K rations, which are packed in flat, waterproof cans, each holding enough concentrated food for one person for one meal. We were given our choice of breakfast, dinner, or supper rations. The supper unit contains a can of cheese flavored with bacon, and breakfast and dinner units consist of varying degrees of blended egg yolk with chipped ham or sausage. The truck drivers had picked up a twenty-gallon can of hot coffee on the way, and Ruthie, always efficient on the food end, ladled it out in canteen cups and empty plasma cans.

We stood knee-deep in mud, in the drizzling rain, eating our cold K on crackers, and watching the GI's clear away the remains of the mess tent.

After breakfast I visited Chester in the ward tent. After having left him the night before with his face hidden by an oxygen mask, I did not recognize the spry, smiling patient, smoking a cigarette and talking to anybody who would listen.

"Who are you, and what do you do?" he asked me as I approached. This was a surprise, as usually it was I who did the interrogating, not the patients. Chester's normal occupation, I found, had been driving a bread truck in Texas, and he hoped the war would end as soon as possible so he could get back to his truck and his girl.

Nurse Betty Cook, her pretty face rather white and her wounded left arm in bandages, was back on duty. She was to be awarded the Purple Heart, as the first nurse to be wounded on Italian soil.*

We climbed into a jeep driven by a Medical Corps man with a red cross painted on the front of his helmet. He was going to take us forward to an ambulance relay point where he would pick up a load of wounded to bring back to the clearing station. As our jeep slithered out of the mud-churned hospital area, the sun broke through with that capriciousness so characteristic of Italian winter weather. We slid through steep carved ruts, while the sky swiftly cleared and the sun sparkled on a road as glossy as chocolate lacquer.

We turned into Highway Number Six and headed directly toward the German-held mountain. Jerry's lofty observation point was fog-bound and seemed to be rising from a bowl of milk. Everything was so still, so pure, that it seemed impossible that from this same mountain such hell could have gushed forth the night before.

As we drove toward the front, in this crystalline light, even the signs of war took on a softened character. The tanks and half-tracks and mules, crowded under olive groves so as to be screened from the air, seemed there for some peaceful purpose. The soldiers peeping out of caves and clustered in sheltered ravines might have been resting during a hiking trip planned by a tourist agency. Ancient villages, hanging like fairy castles in the cliffs, took on such magic in the slanting sun that one forgot that every wall was pockmarked and every roof had crashed into rubble. The Italian landscape became a picture-postcard background for war.

Only the road signs brought back the grim reality. Signs which read MINES CLEARED 20 FEET EACH SIDE gave way, as we drove forward, to signs reading WARNING: MINES NOT CLEARED BEYOND ROAD SHOULDERS. I reflected that it would be many years before Italian mothers could let their children out to play in the fields without fearing for their lives, or before tourists or lovers could wander carelessly through the hills.

But even on this tranquil morning, when it seemed there could be no evil in the world, I kept two cameras open and ready. My Rolleiflex always hung by a strap around my neck, so that any sudden flight to a ditch could not separate me from working equipment. A Speed Graphic

---

* A few weeks later, at Anzio, she became the first woman in the American Army to receive the Bronze Star, "for meritorious service . . . in direct support of combat troops." This made her also the first woman to wear two decorations.

with a telephoto lens rode always on my knees, ready for instantaneous action. As we drove along, I periodically checked the apertures and shutter settings to conform to changing light values. If anything happens, it occurs with such speed that the extra second it takes to open a camera may cost a picture. Both Padgitt and I always kept our pockets filled with extra film, never knowing when the rush of events might separate us from the jeep or when we might come back from a foxhole to find our jeep no longer in existence.

We were driving parallel to a stretch of railroad track where a squad of road engineers was busy clearing away the broken ties and rails, transforming this railroad bed into a second highway which would relieve Number Six of some of the pressure.

We were just crossing a small trestle the engineers had constructed over the framework of the blown-up railroad bridge when I saw, rising straight out of the mountaintop ahead of us, an amazingly tall column shaped like a swiftly growing poplar tree.

"Stop!" I called to the jeep driver. "I want a picture."

"Hold it!" he said. "Jerry's been aiming at this bridge every day for a week now. We don't want to be on it when he starts laying them in again."

By the time we had driven beyond the trestle, the smoke column had vanished, but soon another, and then another grew where the last had been. These ghostly poplars were being planted from our side. We were trying to run Jerry out of his OP with phosphorus shells. I wondered what it was like up there in the little caves and foxholes where the Germans were hiding, with the flaming explosions searing their flesh and setting fire to their clothes, as the phosphorus from each burst kept running into their dugouts like hot quicksilver.

Another mile of driving, and we reached an exquisite arch of ancient masonry which led off Highway Number Six to the right. A Red Cross flag hung over it, marking an ambulance relay point. Here casualties were brought in jeeps, when they could be reached by road, and in litters when they had to be carried directly down the steep mountainsides, to be relayed by ambulance to hospitals in the rear.

We drove through the archway, still miraculously intact, and behind it, as though it had been a Hollywood false front, we found an old stable laid in ruins. Camouflaged under low-hung nets was a cluster of ambulances. Sitting on the rubble piles was a group of badly shaken boys.

These were Medical Corps men, wearing the characteristic helmet painted with a red cross. They were stationed here on thirty-hour relays, and it was their job to go out in response to telephone calls from the front to bring back the wounded.

This had been a painful morning for them. A jeepful of them had just returned with a grim account of a shell hit that had taken place right before their eyes. While their jeep had escaped by a narrow margin, they had watched that shell land on another medical jeep that was crossing a road junction immediately ahead. In that jeep had been three of their gang, including their major. He had been a popular officer, and the boys took it hard.

Also it was disturbing the way Jerry kept concentrating on that particular road junction. These boys at the relay station had to cross that junction every time a phone call summoned them to the front.

It wasn't so much what the boys had to say as what they didn't say that gave me some insight into the way they felt. One of them kept turning the pages of a comic sheet he had received in the mail from home. Another reread old letters. The others sat doing nothing, and saying next to nothing, merely waiting for that phone call which would send them out to the front, over the road junction where they had lost their major, up to meet the litter-bearers at the battalion aid station, to get their load of wounded.

They didn't have to tell me that they were sitting there figuring out how they could outwit the next shell. I could see it written in their faces. It was like guessing heads or tails. If you speed up and cross that junction a little sooner, will you beat the shell there? Or if you go a little more slowly, will it hit the road before you arrive? And if it comes, is it going to be only a stray? Or will it be the first of a barrage?

You hear a lot of the philosophy, "The one that's got my name on it is the one that's going to get me." But I doubt if there is a soldier at the front who isn't trying to outthink that particular shell with his number on it.

The only way to bear the waiting, to endure the constant dread, is to develop a certain numbness which acts as a protective shell. This happens to the boys who must stay for weeks and sometimes months in the forward foxholes. The world around them becomes unreal. The days slip by with their overcurrent of strain and danger. But the Medical Corps men who are litter-bearers and jeep drivers see such concentrated

Army doctors determine their strategy from X-ray films.

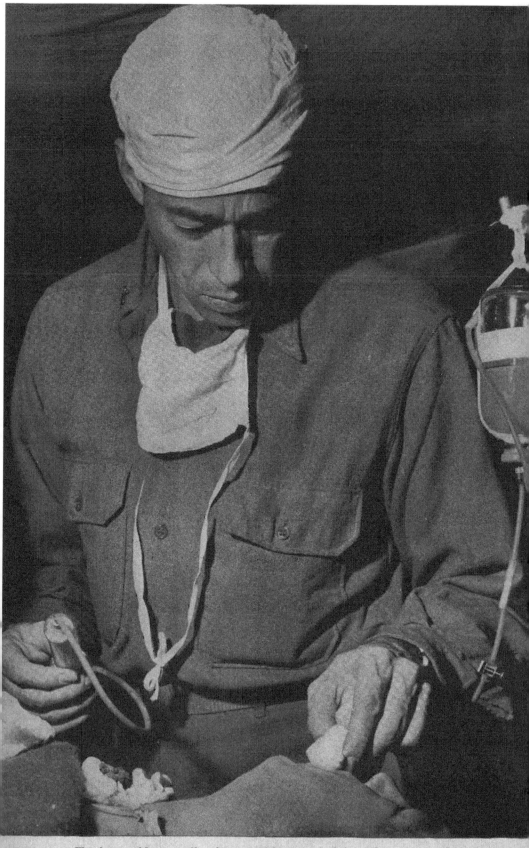

This boy could not swallow because of his wound. Colonel Sanger sponged his dry lips

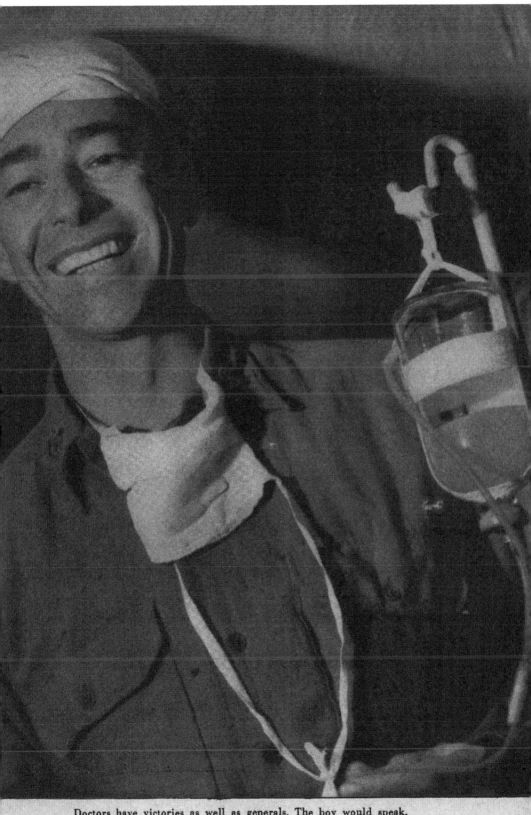

Doctors have victories as well as generals. The boy would speak,
swallow, breathe normally again.

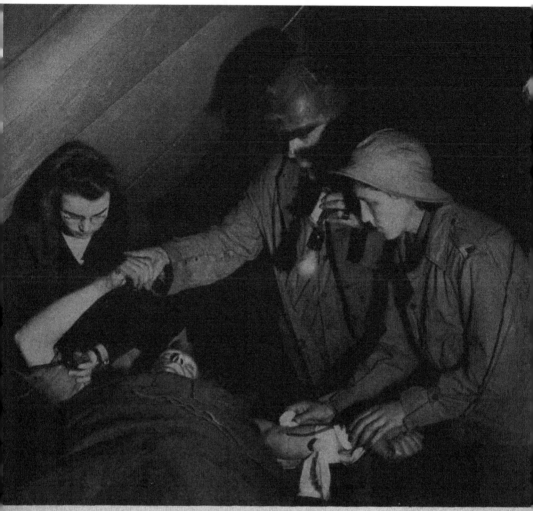

This is, literally, a picture of the shock of battle.

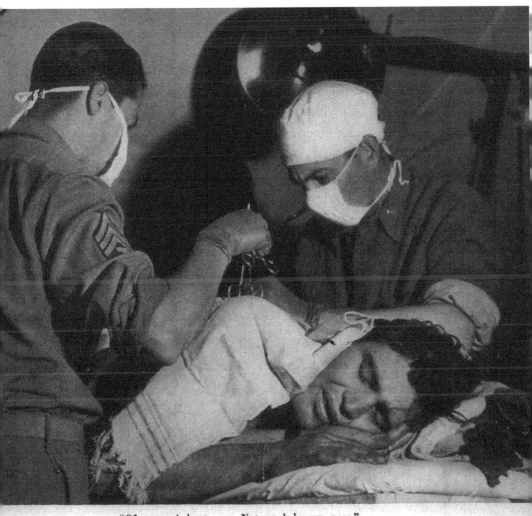

"Of course it hurts, son. Not much longer, now."

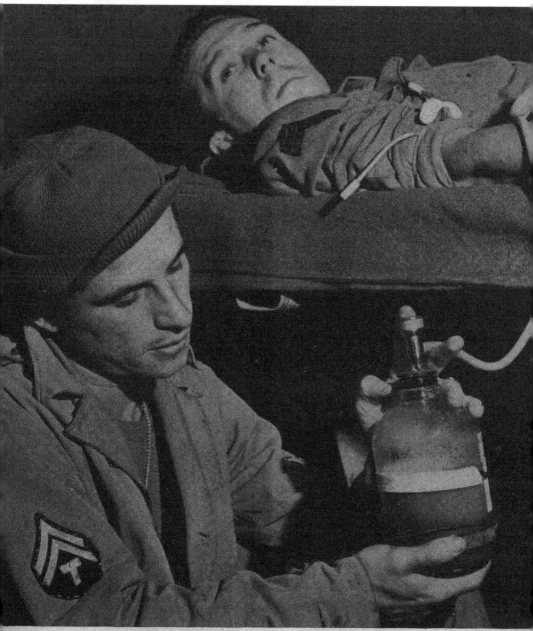

When you know you may need blood yourself tomorrow, you give it freely.

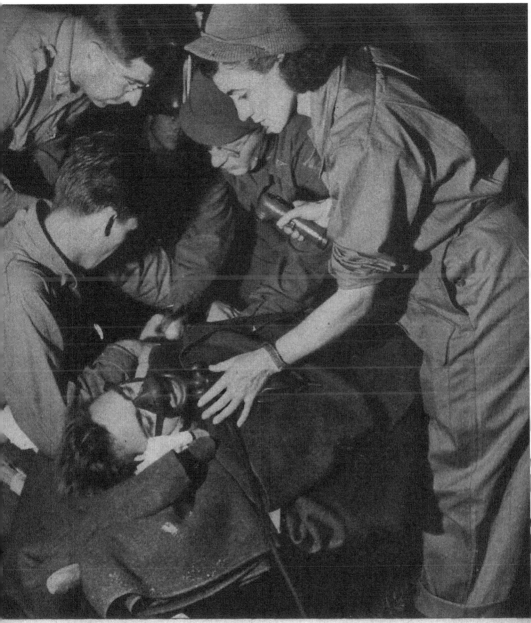

Oxygen is for the desperately wounded, who could not live without it.

Mud wears out ambulances, wears out drivers, wears out litter-bearers,
wears out the wounded.

Many wounded need many ambulances.

Walking mends the convalescent's morale as well as his body . . .

... even in mud.

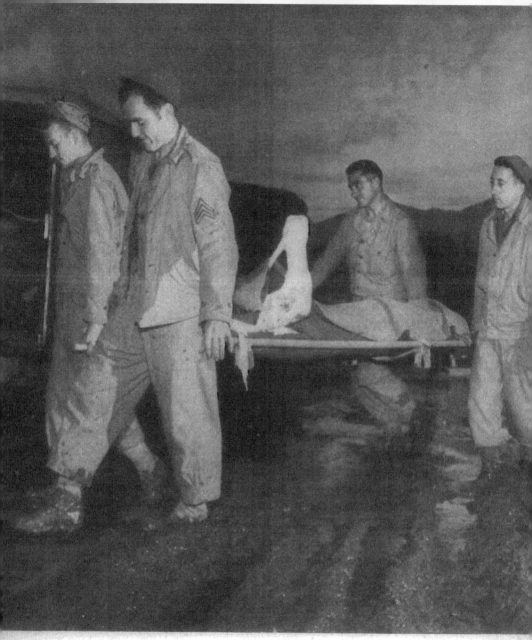

To a surgeon this is great sculpture.

Home is a long hop . . . and a maybe.

They walk in beauty—every damned one of them.

NURSES LATRINE

Wherever there has been a frontier, American women have always been willing
to undergo hardships to stand by their men.

"Clean sheets, too."

results of each battle that even this merciful coat of numbness is impossible for them. Every day they carry casualties who are vivid reminders of what flying steel can do to soft human bodies.

Corporal Padgitt and I took pictures of the corps men as they sat there. Finally the boy who was reading his comic sheet glanced up and said, "It's time for mess. We've got all the K rations you want. Help yourselves. We don't get very hungry up here."

And he went back to his comic strips, reading and rereading the same four pages.

Padgitt and I had just finished a unit each of Dinner K and Breakfast K respectively (the Corporal liked the cheese ration—and no amount of danger could harm his appetite—and I always chose the egg-yolk concoction), when we heard a familiar sound rushing out of the mountain. It was that same crashing sequence we knew so well, like giant feet stalking in our direction. The medical boys grabbed us and rushed us into the ruins of the stable, where we lay in the straw as flat as we could.

Blast after blast sounded. As the echoes of each set of explosions died away, a new series of blasts began. We lay there pressed as tight to the ground as we could get. I remember feeling terribly long. Then I tried to figure out whether I would take up less space if I rolled up in a ball. But I made only a brief try at that, because it makes you feel uncomfortably high in the wrong places. Then I debated whether it was better to keep my helmet more over my face or farther over the back of my neck.

I tried to keep from wondering whether the one wall of the stable which was still standing would come crashing down on us. Then I began puzzling stupidly why the explosions kept on like that, one after another, instead of finally dying away as a barrage of shells usually does. I found that the others were wondering, too, and a few of us crept cautiously to the archway to look.

Fringing the road just opposite us was a curtain of rising gray smoke. "Why, they hit our small-arms ammunition dump!" one of the ambulance drivers exclaimed. The blasts we were listening to were from our own ammunition going up in smoke.

Somehow your own shrapnel doesn't seem so bad. The surprise element is lacking. Padgitt helped me set up shop behind a fragment of the ruined wall, handing me filters and extra film packs as I needed them, and we began photographing the scene ahead, framing it in the archway. It was a remarkable sight; we could get the results of enemy and Allied shelling in one picture. In the foreground were the blackish explosions from our ammo dump which the Germans had hit, and above rose the enemy's mountain with our phosphorus bursts still rising in graceful columns from the peak.

Our ammo dump kept on sputtering for an hour and a half, sending up ugly trails of smoke which stained the sky with a yellowish hue. At the same time, a high overcast began drifting over the sun, and with another of those fickle changes of weather a fine drizzle started sifting down.

The eruptions across the road were beginning to die away when the medical boys got a call to send a jeep forward for wounded. This was a good chance for Padgitt and me to hitchhike our way forward too, so we got into the jeep.

We negotiated the crucial junction quite quietly. Already the ever-present road gangs had filled the shell holes with rubble. At the side of the road, in addition to a few jeep fragments, were the twisted frames of two half-tracks and a 6x6 truck.

An eighth of a mile beyond the junction, our driver turned off Highway Six into a little byroad. We drove through an exquisite grove of evergreens until we reached a deep rockbound crevasse, where the heavy fir boughs created an artificial twilight. Almost invisible under their draperies of camouflage nets was a group of trailers, trucks, and pyramidal tents. This was a tank destroyer command post, the TD-CP, as the abbreviated terminology of the Army goes.

Our medical jeep dropped us here and went on. It was to continue another mile and a half up a steeply winding road to the cross-shaped foxhole which was the Battalion Aid Station, where it would pick up its load of casualties which had been carried on litters down from the lines. The Corporal hunted up somebody who would hunt for the CO.

The CO of the TD's was what is known as Quite a Character. Within my first ten minutes at the post I heard many stories about how his men had to hold him back, during each advance, to keep him from going in ahead of the infantry. In the eleventh minute I was told how he had captured a German single-handed and brought him back to the CP to interrogate him about German gun positions.

In the twelfth minute I was being introduced to the CO himself, a

lively little barrel-shaped man with "old Army colonel" written all
over him. It was less than a quarter of an hour before I had heard the
CO's own account of what wonderful pioneer work was being done by
his beloved tank destroyers.

"We had to make work for ourselves," he said, "figure out new ways
for TD's to be useful." Tank destroyers were not mere machines to him.
They were trail blazers.

A tank destroyer is not a tank, although to the layman it looks like
one. It has armor, and carries a 105-mm. gun, which is used under
normal battle conditions for destroying tanks. However, tanks would
not be effectively employed by either side until the armies got farther
out on the plains. So the TD's were being used as movable gun units.

"I had to figure out something to keep my boys from chewing their
nails," the Colonel explained. "Come into the CP and I'll show you on
the map."

He took me into the HQ trailer, which was suffocating from the heat
of a tiny wood stove, and fitted up like an office, its walls lined with
maps.

"We're reversing all the rules in this Italian campaign," he said.
"Here we actually have artillery ahead of the infantry."

He pointed to a spot on the map, beyond Mignano, the road leading
toward Cassino. "See that little curve around Highway Six? It took
weeks of fighting for us to work our way around that horseshoe. It's still
so hot that it would be foolish to bring infantry along it."

He sketched out the front lines for me on the map. "Our artillery
combed and searched and crisscrossed all the areas in front of the infantry. And now the troops have spread out into the hills to the right
and left. But the horseshoe is being held by our tank destroyers."

I could understand why he was so proud: it was a kind of pioneering
to use tank destroyers as mobile gun positions.

"The horseshoe gets so much plastering that we had to bring our
TD's around it in the dark. That curve of Six is our most advanced position in the Fifth Army, as of today. At the end of the horseshoe is our
most forward TD."

I could see the missionary gleam in his eye.

"My, I'd like to take a picture of that tank destroyer," I said.

"Well, that's really the front, you know," said the Colonel. "Beyond
that lies no man's land."

"I've always wanted to take a picture of no man's land," I said, not quite truthfully, because until that moment the idea had never popped into my head.

"We'll see. We'll see," said the Colonel. "I have to go up there, anyway, tomorrow to make sure things are going all right. We'll see how the Heinies are laying them in."

While we were looking at the maps, a major of the armored division had taken down the field telephone which hung in its leather case on the wall of the trailer. Snatches of conversation drifted our way.

"Do you have any report from your forward platoons?" the Major was asking.

"He's getting all the dope from forward so we can make plans for sending out our night patrols," the Colonel explained.

"Here's the thing," the Major was saying. "The Colonel wants you to keep alerted, because last night there were two enemy patrols trying to infiltrate. Be sure to keep your people alerted."

"Ask them, how about artillery?" the Colonel broke in.

"Much stuff being dropped in there?" the Major questioned. "Can you make any guess as to the size of it? Is it direct fire?"

Evidently it was direct fire, for the Major replied, "That's tough!" The boys hate most the direct fire from the German high-velocity guns, for the shell lands before they can hear it scream. It's always the first high-velocity shell that gets some of our men because there is no warning for them to scatter into foxholes.

"Tell them to be prepared to move the battery," the Colonel broke in, and then added, "Tell them to talk to the Time and Space man." *

"The Colonel wants you to talk to the Time and Space man. Austin is the Time and Space man. Well, so long, pal. Be sure to keep us posted if the situation changes any up there."

The Major slipped the telephone back into its case.

I always admired these field telephones, in their smart tan leather cases. You held a button open with your finger while you talked, which snapped the circuit automatically closed when you finished, to conserve the batteries. Someone with imagination had picked the names of the telephone exchanges: words like Lightning, Rapid, Speedy.

"Time to put on the feedbag," said the Colonel, and we went out into

* The individual who calculates the complex problem of the time required for the specific movement of tank destroyers under existing conditions—"road net," availability of fuel, possible congestion.

the drizzling twilight and filed through a narrow fern-filled gorge to an open tent half which sheltered a board table. Mess was early; it was only five o'clock, but it was important to eat while we still had a little daylight, as we dared not use flashlights under the open canvas.

In the half-darkness several officers were seated around the plank table, laughing heartily. As we entered, I heard just enough of the conversation to know they were retelling the story of the celebrated buck private at Salerno, when they recognized me and stopped abruptly.

"Don't worry," I said, "I've heard that one before."

The tale, which had been gleefully related to me some weeks back by a second lieutenant claiming to be an eyewitness, was about a soldier who landed in the advance wave, and at the end of the first furious hour on the beachhead came up to ask where the prophylactic station was.

For supper we had the usual choice of K: breakfast, dinner, or supper ration. We each took some of all three, making what looked like a cold stew in our mess kits, with the various egg-yolk compounds and baconized cheese, which we ate with the hard crackers that come in the K-ration tins.

During supper I heard more about tanks and tank destroyers. It was the tank boys, I was told, who were really "sweating it out." There had been occasional attempts to bring up tanks where they could be used effectively, like the one I had seen from the air when flying with Captain Marinelli, but the Jerries just sat up in their OP's and blasted them off the road as they came around the bend, like boys at a fair picking off mechanical ducks one at a time.

Our men had quite a time evacuating those tanks. Salvage squads brought them back for repair, but cleaning them out was the worst. "It is not much fun," I was told, "to climb into a tank and find the crew in such little bits you can't recognize them."

There was a good deal more along these lines, and some of it was pretty hard-boiled talk. But I realized that referring to death and wounds in the somewhat whimsical fashion these men frequently adopted did not mean that they had become calloused. On the contrary, each time more of their comrades were lost, they became angrier and more eager to punish the enemy. But the only way to bear the constant presence of danger seemed to be to talk about it lightly.

"I'll never forget the time they brought in those two fellows who had been shooting a bazooka," one of the officers continued. "One of them was hit in his pocket; and he had been carrying around his shaving brush. Did they have a swell time at the hospital picking out all those brush hairs!"

"That's what you call a close shave," contributed the Major, for which he got the razz from the whole table.

From this point the discussion reached that inevitable debate: do you hear the shell that hits you? As long as I traveled in heavy gun circles I was to hear this problem endlessly discussed. It was never solved to everybody's satisfaction, but it usually ended up with someone affirming positively, "Well, I claim that the one that gets you you never hear!"

After mess, I was conducted to a contrivance of which the men were as proud as of their TD's. It was a shower bath, and it was being turned over to me for my exclusive use.

When we reached it, they pushed me through a small muddy hole in the side of a hill, and then went away politely and left me to my own devices. The hole was thickly surrounded with exquisite maidenhair ferns which hung over it like a fringe. Inside, a cavelike pit had been dug out of the earth, just deep enough so that to get my feet to the bottom I had to let myself down by my hands from tree roots. In its murky interior I propped up my GI flashlight, hung my clothes on a small root, and swung a five-gallon can from a larger tree root, where it had been filled with water and roped to a primitive swivel device. Insofar as my aim was correct, I would receive a complete shower bath. I aimed carefully and pulled. After negotiating this, I put on my clothes. I suppose I was technically cleaner. I was certainly muddier.

It was completely dark when I climbed out of the mudbank. I worked my way through the slippery gorge and, tripping over camouflage nets here and there, finally located the CP trailer. Inside it was bright and warm from the little wood stove.

The Colonel was on the telephone, directing the front patrols. "I don't believe those people down there are alive to the danger they're in. I think their line is out. Get a recon out. Be pretty hard to get them on the radio and tell them all the things you need to.

"It's a pretty wet night. Better send a combined patrol. Even as dark as it is, better not drive a jeep.

"Get past the junction, do some listening. Remain thirty minutes and come back. I want a report as soon as you return."

He replaced the telephone, which was immediately taken over by the

Major, who phoned through to the head of the horseshoe to get in touch with the mule skinners. "How many mules have we got on the dead-line?" he inquired. Meanwhile the CO turned to maps to explain to me about mules.

Mules are as valuable as guns in this mountainous warfare in Italy. Under cover of darkness, mule trains go up the rocky slopes to troops which cannot be reached by jeeps, carrying food and ammunition supplies. Sometimes the terrain is so rough that the men must even leave the mules behind, and carry up supplies on their shoulders. But always our soldiers are fed no matter how great the difficulties. The CO pointed out one spot on the map on a forward rocky slope where enemy fire was so heavy that one of his boys got pinned to a foxhole for eleven days. He was within sight of his comrades, but the intervening hundred-foot stretch was so hot, both day and night, that no one could carry him his rations. They solved the problem by tossing him a ration can every few hours, until on the twelfth day he was freed by an infantry advance.

These forward positions were pointed out to me on a remarkable series of maps. The maps, I knew, were turned out in a steady stream by the Engineering Corps, from small offset presses on trailers brought up close behind the lines and operated by the "Typo Unit." These typographical charts showed detailed elevation data, treeless and wooded areas, and the numerous mule trails. The maps interested me particularly because it happens that my father, who was an engineer and inventor of printing machinery, was responsible for designing the first eight small printing presses on trucks to be brought to the front lines with the American Army in France in World War I. These presses printed daily charts from photographs made by reconnaissance planes, and in the First World War this was considered revolutionary.

It was after midnight when the Colonel received the call for which he was waiting, from the returning patrols.

"Did they draw any fire during the movement?" we heard him ask. "That's very good."

And then he listened further. "Lantern or something burning in a house?" And then: "Have they reported any mines around that area? . . . Did they explode it? . . . Oh, I see, disarmed it. . . . Well, I think it's mighty fine work, pal. Glad you made those changes. Be sure and keep us posted if anything further happens up there." And he hung up.

"There were German patrols attempting to infiltrate past the horseshoe," the Colonel told us. "Some came past at ten and some after twelve. One of our boys heard them pass so close that he could hear them whispering in German. There's some reshuffling going on."

It was as hard for me to leave this direct wire to the front as to put down a detective story, but it was time to go to bed.

The Major led me out into the darkness and established me in a trailer where I was to spend the night. The boys had outdone themselves with my "boudoir," just as they had with my private shower bath. They had lifted out the ammo, or whatever it had previously contained, and blown up an air mattress for the floor of the truck, and put my bedroll over it. One of the standard five-gallon water tins had been placed by my bedroll, so I could wash in my helmet.

I undressed in total darkness; even my small pencil flash could not be used in the truck because the camp must maintain complete blackout. As usual it was something of an achievement to pour water from the heavy GI can into my helmet without tipping it over. I assisted the operation by propping the helmet between my heavy GI boots.

I had spent nights in foxholes sleeping in my bedroll on the ground. Once in the bottom of a dugout I had been given a door to sleep on, salvaged from a ruined farmhouse near by; and that door had been a luxury. So my present quarters seemed very fine indeed.

I lay in the darkness and listened to the hoarse voices of the guns speaking to the enemy and echoing rhythmically through the hills. The sky brightened and darkened as the muzzle flashes from near-by artillery blazed forth periodically and then died away. At regular intervals I could hear the footsteps of the sentry, just beyond my trailer. Sometimes I could hear his low voice:

"Halt! Who's there?"

And the quiet answer, "An officer of the post."

"Come forward and be recognized," the guard would say.

And then I could just catch the exchange of passwords.

"Angus," said the sentry.

"Bull," replied the officer.

The night before the challenge had been "Jersey," and the response had been not "cow" as one might expect, but "Bounce."

The password is changed every night, and the selection is made on the basis of two words with enough connection to be easily remembered, but not so obvious that anyone can guess it. There is no fooling with passwords. The sentry is empowered to shoot at the feet of anyone who does not have the correct response.

I recalled a story about a recent password. An officer got out of a jeep at an armored division CP and approached the sentry in front of the headquarters tent. "Advance to be recognized!" said the sentry, and then spoke the challenge, "Pennsylvania."

"Railroad," answered the officer.

"Well, I guess that's close enough," said the sentry.

The correct password had been "Pennsylvania Station," but as the officer stepped forward, the sentry had recognized General Mark Clark.

CHAPTER 15

At the End of the Horseshoe

TODAY WAS to be an important day. I was to have my wish; I was to be taken to the front. I lay there in the trailer, watching the sky grow lighter and wondering what the front would look like.

Just before I had left the Colonel the night before, still telephoning to his patrols, he had told me that unless any unexpected action developed he would show me his forward TD positions and take me around the horseshoe.

In rough terminology, I was already at "the front." The front is, loosely speaking, a band of about six miles wide, bordering on enemy territory, filled with our artillery and infantry activity, and within range of enemy fire. During the last twelve weeks I had done a good deal of work in these forward areas. But today would be different. On this day I was to be taken to the edge of no man's land.

While it is on the whole very pleasant to be a woman war correspondent, there is always the possibility that you will be protected too much. Sometimes Army officers forget that it is just as necessary for you to get your work done as it is for a male correspondent—that you are responsible for turning out the same work. But I have noticed over and over that the closer you are to the actual fighting lines, the more freedom you are given, and the more opportunities. In the forward areas both officers and men are glad to see someone who is taking an interest in what they are doing, and everyone helps you enthusiastically to get the news and the pictures.

It was light by now, although the sky was still a foggy gray. Padgitt knocked on my trailer door, with a fresh five-gallon can of water.

"How was your boudoir?" he asked.

"Fine," I said. "What kind of quarters did you get?"

The Corporal was bubbling over because he had run into an old friend whom he hadn't seen since his school days in Des Moines. In telling about it he broke into one of his rare bursts of speech. "We slept in a dugout so small that the mice had to put up one-way traffic signs. We were so close together that when I reached into my pocket for my cigarettes I pulled out my buddy's pack, and when I started to put my helmet on, I got it on his head. Well, it was small!"

For Padgitt, this was being garrulous.

I spent the morning taking pictures around the CP, and after mess the Colonel was ready to take me to the front.

"We'll take only one jeep forward," he said. "They don't always bother to shoot at one jeep."

Padgitt was packing my equipment back of my seat, when the Colonel said, "I don't think we should expose any more men than absolutely necessary. I'll help you if you need any assistance with your cameras at the front."

I could see the disappointed look on the Corporal's face. I knew he had wanted to see no man's land as much as I.

"Do you mind riding with the top down in the rain?" the Colonel asked. "We'll see more. And then we can roll out faster if we have to."

I was more than willing to ride with the top down in the rain. The Corporal lent me his raincoat to tuck around the cameras and films. My Rolleiflex, from which I was never parted, hung around my neck, protected by a trench coat.

We started up the jeep, and Padgitt spoke another of his infrequent sentences: "Do you have your portable foxhole with you?" Then we were off.

The rain was coming down in spoonfuls as we swung out into Highway Number Six and started along that last two miles to the front. A front-line road has a character of its own. Driving forward, every quarter of a mile has a kind of increased significance. No one has to tell you that the enemy is near. If you were lifted out of lower Broadway and suddenly placed there, you would feel the presence of the enemy through the pores of your skin.

You become sensitized to topography. A general, I suppose, is someone who can comprehend the strategic meaning of geography, but to the individual the landscape takes on a personal intensity. Every little knoll is something you can hide behind. Every open stretch of road is something unfriendly. A deep little ditch, especially if there is no water at the bottom of it, is something for which you have an instant, instinctive fondness. The landscape becomes as intimate as the features of someone you love.

As we drove forward, I was surprised to see what a crowded place the front is. Every olive tree screened a jeep or half-track. Every open space had its ack-ack gun. Bordering the road shoulders were shell holes round enough to have been cut with a cookie cutter. Every gully was as cluttered as the backstage of a musty vaudeville house, its camouflaged rifle or howitzer under netting sewn with rag leaves like cheap scenery. Dozens of soldiers crowded every ravine, watching and waiting. Every acre was so jammed with people and with heavy machinery that the front looked like the furniture department in a bargain basement.

"There's so much artillery up here," said the Colonel, "that it's practically packed hub to hub."

The most striking sight of all were the communications lines. I had never seen such telephone wires. They crept over the rocks like cobwebs, followed the edges of ruined walls, spread over the rubble of crumbled farmhouses in great fans. Sometimes fifty strands were tied loosely together in careless knots. Sometimes they ran along the grass and shrubs like threads traveling over the bed of a weaving machine. The Signal Corps worked at night, carrying their communications lines forward under shell fire. The men sometimes had to swim streams in the dark to mend breaks caused by enemy shelling. The telephone has become a major military weapon. Every command post, every observation point, every gun position needs its telephone.

In the course of our forward trip, there were frequent intervals when we had to be watchful to keep from tripping over these telephone lines. This is when we plunged from the jeep and ran off the road—for we did what the Colonel referred to each time it happened as "plain and fancy diving into ditches"; but the incoming shells were sporadic and brief.

"This is like the old Indian wars," the Colonel rambled on, as we drove forward. "This is a war of concealment. The fellow who stays out of sight the most is the one who lives the longest. The Hun is better at it than we are. It's the law of self-preservation, I guess. He's been at it longer. Until we learned the game of hiding, Americans got killed awfully easy."

We passed a line of cypress trees lying flat on the ground in an orderly row. They had been cut off at the ankles by shells hitting the road which they had guarded for the past century like a rank of old-fashioned soldiers. Nobody had told them that this was a war of concealment.

The Colonel drew the jeep off the road and parked it in the shelter of a knob-shaped stony hill. "The Germans are just on the other side of this hill," he told me. "But first I want you to see Bessie."

I didn't have a chance to ask him who Bessie was, because he began pulling himself up through the slippery rocks like a schoolboy on a holiday, and it was all I could do to follow and keep my camera dry under my trench coat.

Soon we were skirting the rim of a bowl-shaped rocky hollow, a depression in the side of the hill. The sides of this natural crater were split with cracks and little caves, and I realized that from all these crevasses we were being watched by dozens of eyes.

The Colonel paused to explain to me that the security section, part of the TD platoon, was stationed here, and spent the daytime hidden in the crater. Some of his telephone messages the night before had been to this group. These boys were on watch at night to prevent infiltration by enemy infantry. They listened for any sounds of activity on foot. German patrols made a practice of slipping through the lines at night, attempting to overpower and capture our gunners; the security section stood guard to protect our gun crews from being taken by surprise while they were either sleeping or shooting.

I thought of the Colonel's comment that this was like the Indian wars, for the security boys looked as though they were playing Indian, as they peeped out of their cave entrances at us. To them as I stood there in my GI boots and leggings, Army trousers, dripping trench coat and helmet, I must have looked very much like any other GI. Suddenly I heard one of them exclaim, "Holy smoke! The Old Man's got a chicken with him." After that they were speechless until another one found his tongue and volunteered that I was the first woman they had seen for three months.

I took a few pictures at the cave entrances. The boys who were lucky enough to have cards were playing poker (there was more cash than cards at the front—the boys had no way to spend their money). One lad, who roomed alone in a crack of rock so narrow that there was barely space for one man in it, had a little dog who sat on his chest. It was the second dog I had met in forty-eight hours named Sad Sack.

The Colonel led me on up the hill to meet Bessie, who turned out to be an M 10 tank destroyer. Her name was neatly lettered on the carriage of her three-inch gun. Beside Bessie lay the ruins of her predecessor, a German 75-mm. high-velocity gun.

"The Heinies knew a good gun position when they saw one," said the destroyer crew. "It was just bang-scream-wham the whole time that high-velocity was here. It gets your goat! We had a devil of a job prying them out of here."

"They did a neat job of souping it up," said another gunner, indicating the wreckage of slats and beams that had been used to camouflage the 75. "We lifted a dead Kraut out of there yesterday so he wouldn't smell up the landscape. But don't go poking around. That mess hasn't had the boobies taken out of it yet."

From where we stood, we could not see into German territory. Bessie had been installed where she would be hidden by the last few feet of hilltop. But we could look back from our high position and see miles of Highway Number Six stretching in the direction from which we had come. It was this gleaming band of ribbon over which our boys had bled and fought, inching their way through months of pain. Far into the distance I could see our motor convoys crawling along at regularly spaced intervals, like roaches on a wet strip of glass. But beyond the hill on which I stood, most of the vehicles did not go, because the next stretch of road was the famous "horseshoe."

As we climbed down the hill toward our jeep, the Colonel told me that he would take me first just over the arm of the curve as far as our most forward OP. There we would stop and see how things were before completing the trip around the horseshoe.

"Jerry has certain habits," the Colonel explained. "He'll start in at certain times and go dotting right across the valley. You get to learn his habits. Sometime he'll cross us up. The day he crosses us up, a bunch of people will get killed."

He looked at his watch. It was 3:15. "This isn't such a bad time. He always starts in around four o'clock. Then falls off a little. And then just about 5:15, at dusk, he'll start peppering them in again."

We drove around the hill and suddenly the whole length of the horseshoe was in sight. I was amazed that this brief loop of road could have cost so many lives. I could have walked along it, lighting a cigarette at the beginning and still have had a puff left for the end.

Almost immediately the Colonel swung off into a little protected rocky enclosure. Parked there were an armored personnel carrier and a half-track M2 for artillery fire control. The M2 had the name *Dimples* lettered on the hood and it was equipped with radio to relay the findings of the observation post. At a slight elevation in the cliff at our backs was the opening to a tiny cave. This was our forward OP, and at the mouth of the cave were three observers with binoculars.

"Jumpin' Jupiter!" said one of the boys, as he lowered his binoculars. "The Colonel's got a doll in the jeep."

"This is *Life*, come to take your pictures," said the Colonel.

They were too surprised to talk at first, but while I set my cameras, they found their voices. They were immensely excited about having their pictures taken. "We'll be talking about this for days," said Sergeant Hipskind, their youngster of a radio operator, who wore a little pointed beard. "Nothing ever happens up here. There's nothing to do but sit in an OP all day and watch your watch."

They were flooding me now with questions about home. How was food rationing? Could you still get steaks? How was it about gas? Was it really as bad as people said?

"I'd love to go home and test out some of these hardships they're talking about," remarked one of the observers.

"Jerry been laying them in lately?" the Colonel inquired.

"Not for the last fifty minutes, sir," said the boys. But an hour ago, they told us, a jeep rounding the horseshoe caught a burst. It killed the driver, and shrapnel got one man in the lungs and another in the hand. The casualties had been rushed back to the rear.

"Has anyone come to clean out that cave yet?" the Colonel asked the observers. "No, sir," was the reply. I realized that they were referring to the fact that the cave had not yet been examined for mines.

All through the journey the Colonel had been picking out places where he could deposit me if shelling started. He took a pair of binoculars from one of the boys and started scanning the landscape, meanwhile remarking to me, "Don't wander too far away. If they start lobbing them in I'm going to put you right in that cave."

"How about the mines?" I asked.

"We'll have to take a chance on the mines," he replied. I thought this an interesting choice.

It was odd to stand there, in the loop of the horseshoe, with the uneasy consciousness that German observers were looking toward us through their binoculars.

"You're closer to the front than any woman has ever been," said the Colonel. "You're ahead of the infantry. But our most forward TD is at the end of the horseshoe. If you want a picture of that, I'll take you."

Well, I wanted it.

It was still raining, but the fog was lifting, enough, I thought, to take photographs.

"Do you think you can take pictures from the jeep?" the Colonel asked.

Yes, I could, if he didn't mind stopping it.

"It's O.K.," he said, "if we don't have to stop too long. I'm just going to trust to motion to get us out if we have to get going in a hurry."

"If it's a very important picture," I asked, "would you be able to stop the motor for a second?"

"Yes," he said, "if it's only for a second."

We climbed into the jeep. "Good luck," said the observers, and one of them added facetiously, "So nice to have known you."

We started around the curve in the rain and mist, with the uncomfortable certainty that we were being watched by enemy eyes. We seemed to be taking the trip in slow motion. We passed the remains of the jeep that had been blown off the road. Then we passed the rain-soaked body of an Italian civilian by the side of a low wall. "He looks as though he's been dead for several days," said the Colonel. "It's so hot here nobody's bothered to pull him in."

We reached the far end of the horseshoe and there was the tank destroyer, then the most forward Allied position on the European continent. It was partially shielded by the ruins of a most thoroughly shelled farmhouse. It was draped with a camouflage net looking characteristically like an abandoned piece of tattered stage scenery. Crouched beside it, hiding in the rubble from enemy view, were four very wet-looking soldiers.

The Colonel stopped the jeep for a photograph, and cut the motor just in time for us to hear them exclaim, "Jeepers, it's a pigeon!"

As I leaned out to take a picture, one of them said, "You're a long way from home."

"So are you," I replied.

"You ain't kidding!" they called back in chorus.

Beyond us lay the deserted stretch which was no man's land. One thousand yards down the road were the Germans. Just visible through the rain ran Highway Six, deep in enemy territory, skirting Mt. Trocchio, curving past Cassino, and disappearing into the mist on its way to Rome.

"Can you give me a chance to take a picture down the road straight toward the Germans?" I asked.

"Yes," said the Colonel, "but let me get the jeep turned round first so I can head it back."

Once the jeep was turned around, he cut the motor for an instant while I leaned out in the rain and took my picture. It wouldn't be much of a picture, because it was raining so hard.

"I don't suppose I could use a flash bulb here," I said. "It would help a little, with the light so bad."

"Go ahead," said the Colonel, "and make it quick."

I made it quick, and back around the horseshoe we went.

We slowed down as we passed the OP, for the observers were waving to us. "Good-by, *Life*," they called, "good of you to visit us." And within the next minute we were out of sight of the Germans, rounding Mt. Lungo, and cut off temporarily from direct enemy observation.

Something new had been brought up during our journey around the horseshoe. It was a line of pack mules, looking very sad and wet, with dripping reels of telephone wire strapped to their backs. The mule train was waiting in the shelter of Mt. Lungo until after dark, when the Signal Corps men would go up the mountainsides, laying their communications lines. Each mule carried strapped to its side, in addition to its load of wire, a rifle and a set of small entrenching tools. The short-handled spades and picks were for the mule skinners to dig foxholes wherever they might pause on the mountain slopes.

Making a kind of umbrella of my trench coat, and using flash bulbs because the rain was blinding, I photographed the mules.

"You see, we don't take the mules over the horseshoe by daylight," the Colonel commented. "Mules are very valuable."

I said nothing at all.

"A single mule would draw a devil of a lot of fire." His brown eyes were twinkling at me. "We take good care of our mules."

Well, I thought, that certainly puts a war correspondent in her place.

CHAPTER 16

155-mm. Flash Bulb

EVEN IN the daytime the battery CP was always in a half twilight. It had been dug deep in the earth and was lighted by candles melted onto distinctive holders—jagged pieces of shrapnel. These were not just any flak fragments. Each piece, I was to learn, was one to which some crew member had a personal attachment because it had missed him.

When I crawled down into the dugout, the gun computer, a young lad who had grown an amazing mustache, looked up from his chart, his eyes popping.

"Jees," he exclaimed. "We'd heard that a lady had been seen taking pictures from foxholes, but we didn't believe it. Do my eyes deceive me?"

"Wake up," said another boy. "This is *Life* goes to a party with Long Toms. Isn't that the idea?" he asked, turning to me.

"Something like that," I replied. "I thought it might be nice to be at the sending end of artillery instead of the receiving end for a change."

"We can't guarantee that you'll see only the sending end of things tonight," they explained. "We never can tell when we'll get counterbattery."

Counterbattery is a matter of answering back at the enemy. Whenever you can spot his gun position you aim at his battery and try to wash him out. He does the same to you. Counterbattery is a game that both sides can play.

"We've been under a lucky star lately," said the battery executive. "It's a month since we've written any names on shells."

"What do you mean, writing names on shells?" I inquired.

"We have a custom in our battalion," the battery executive explained. "When the Krauts fire counterbattery, and we lose any men, we write the names of the men we have lost on the very next shell we fire."

Lieutenant Robert Maxwell, the battery executive, was a wide-browed young man with pleasant dark eyes. He was sitting in the midst of a mass of wiring and field telephones on a kind of earth bench which had been carved out of the ground and ran completely around the dugout.

"We have to have a telephone to each separate gun," he explained to me, "because the Long Toms are set so far apart that the crews can't hear shouted commands. With a battery of smaller guns, the commands come in direct to a phone by the guns and are shouted for all the crews to hear. Our CP here is a relay post from the Fire Direction Center to the guns."

He picked up a phone and started a kind of incantation into it. "Battery adjust. Shell HE. Charge Super. Fuse quick. Base deflection: left two-six-niner. On number two, close three; battery one round, quadrant five eight zero."

"Sounds like double talk," I said as he hung up.

"Those are the commands for Abel battery," said Lieutenant Maxwell. "Now we're just firing harassing fire at Highway Six toward the end of the Valley. But tonight, when you take pictures, we're going to be trying to knock out a certain bridge we've got designs on, just in front of Cassino."

I had met A for Abel before, in the word alphabet used by artillery. I knew that in the same battalion there would be a B for Baker and a C for Charlie battery, each with its four 155-mm. rifles.

"We'll have just time to show you a round before mess," said the Lieutenant. "You'll be interested in seeing how the Fire Direction Center works."

The FDC, 500 yards away, was the nerve center for the big guns. The enemy was always trying to knock out your FDC, I was told, and you were always trying to do the same with his. But a Fire Direction Center was always hard to find.

This one was located in the deep cellar of a ruined farmhouse which, if seen by enemy air observers, would look like nothing more than a frozen splash of stone. Inside, the cellar had an academic look, in keeping with the higher mathematics employed there. Its scholarly appearance came from its furniture of little school desks which the boys had brought from a half-ruined schoolhouse just up the road.

One desk was shared by the Abel computer and the Baker computer. At the next sat the Charlie and the ammunition computers. Opposite the computers, and facing them over a desk full of charts and transparent deflection fans, were two men carrying the august titles of Vertical Control Operator and Horizontal Control Operator. By an odd coincidence all the computers and control operators in this FDC came from Milwaukee except the Charlie computer, who was from Fort Wayne. Consulting a Fire Possibilities Chart this band of Milwaukeans and the lone Hoosier assigned the guns to each fire mission which could best reach the target. By the use of their computers, or deflection fans, as they were called, plus more mathematics than most of us ever had to learn in college, they worked out the vertical and horizontal shift of guns and tied in the guns for range.

By the time this tight little midwest group got through with their range and deflection calculations, a mere spot on the map where the Germans had a juicy target like a tank park, or a nest of mortars, was translated into a firing command for the Battery CP, and in no time at all a battery of Long Toms was blasting away at it.

"Almost time for chow," said Lieutenant Maxwell. "We'll have just enough time for a visit to the Counter-Battery Section."

We climbed out of the cellar and over the sandbags and piles of rubble and made our way up the side of a steep, rocky hill. Almost hidden in a thick olive grove near the summit was a dilapidated pink plaster farmhouse. An outside stairway led up to the second floor. We paused on the upper landing for a few moments to take in the superb view it afforded of Cassino valley.

Every little while a shell from guns emplaced behind us swept over our heads with a roar, and if we watched carefully for a full minute we could see something that looked like a ripe cotton boll disengaging itself from the far end of the valley floor and rising until it dissolved in the air.

"Routine harassing fire," said the Lieutenant. "Just enough shells on the highway to make things inconvenient for the Jerry supply lines." And we went indoors.

I was always amazed at the number of typewriters and filing cabinets that could be found in a combat zone. The Counter-Battery Section looked like any well-run office, except that its personnel all worked with their helmets on. Also, a certain aura was lent to the filing room by the presence of the Family Willms.

Before the Americans pushed their way into this territory, the Germans had used this same pink farmhouse as an infantry CP. Some would-be artist had found the stretch of plaster wall irresistible, and the result had been a mural-size rendering in charcoal of Nazi home life. When the Germans were forced to retreat, they left the Family Willms behind.

Mama Willms (each figure was captioned) was large and terrifying. Papa Willms was so small and frightened that one wondered if he were a true representative of the Aryan home life which the boys had left behind. Baby Willms was any baby who needed to be housebroken. In the mural, which covered the whole Counter-Battery Section's wall, Mama was making Papa attend to a certain ritual which one usually considers the province of the distaff side. It made one wonder about home life among the Nazis.

Under this scene of Teutonic domesticity was stationed what the artillerymen called the Hostile Battery Historical File. Here, as neatly as though it had been filed in the Library of Congress, records were kept of everything that happened to every known battery of the enemy. For months back, and reaching to the present minute, reports were filed on every location we made of an enemy gun, every time we shot at it, every time it shot at us. Data were collected on enemy artillery all over the front lines. Information was turned in from forward observers, from Cub pilots in flying OP's, from Sound and Flash Battalions, who computed the distance of hostile guns by measuring on a tape the lapse of time from the instant the flash was spotted until the sound was heard. Our Counter-Battery Section co-operated with the British on their left and the French on their right to build their Historical File.

They examined all fragments of enemy shells they could collect. Doughboys were urged to turn in for analysis flak falling near them. By the width of the rotating band (the part that engages in the rifling and gives the shell its twist) they could get the range of the enemy gun and estimate its location.

This list of enemy guns is consulted before an attack, and firing is done on the Counter-Battery Section's recommendations. Immediately before and during an attack, our artillery attempts to silence these known enemy positions, so as to protect advancing infantry as much as possible.

Through the Hostile File, we learned as much about the enemy's firing habits as a diagnostician knows about his patients. The Germans are fond of using a roving gun, which they shoot from one position and rush through a camouflaged road to an alternate point, hoping we will waste a lot of shells on the first location where it is spotted. They go to enormous trouble to conceal this connecting road. Knowing through our files where these positions are, we never waste shells on a roving gun unless we actually see it in place.

But there is one type of hostile gun at which the Counter-Battery Section advises our gunners not to shoot. Every once in a while, through their cross-filing system, the Counter-Battery experts discover that the enemy is firing inaccurately into an area where we have no troops. Then they just let him go ahead and shoot.

After this lesson in enemy-artillery psychology we went down into the cellar of the pink farmhouse, which had been made into a mess hall, and ate C rations, dehydrated potatoes and stewed pears for supper. It was beginning to grow dark, and time to load up cameras and guns. I had planned to work all night with the heavy artillery, because I wanted to learn what a night in the life of a gun crew was like.

"Hope you don't have an artillery duel," said the mess sergeant as we started out of the cellar.

"Hope you're quick at getting into foxholes," wished the KP, "or you'll get dents in your helmet."

When we reached Number 2 gun in Abel battery, the first thing the Lieutenant did was to show me the nearest foxhole, in case I should need it in a hurry, and then I was introduced to the gun crew.

I had seldom seen people more thrilled about having their pictures taken. It seemed to them too good to be true that their own battery, for which they had an almost human affection, had been selected for photographs. They had worked with these 155's throughout the whole Italian campaign, and had named their battery Superman.

"How'd you come to pick our battery?" they asked. Usually these choices are the result of chance, but this time there had been a reason. It had been the idea of the Grasshopper pilots, who had been flying me from spot to spot during my work at the Italian front, to arrange for me to photograph the same battery whose smoke puffs I had caught in my pictures over Cassino valley. This was the battery with which Captain Marinelli had been in communication the day I had flown his mission with him, and it was these very Long Toms which had knocked out the German *Nebelwerfer*. Although Superman had moved periodically forward every time our troops had made an appreciable advance, Captain Marinelli was still air-liaison officer for the battalion.

As I ran around getting cameras ready, the boys warned me that there were two types of stakes I should stay away from. The first were aiming stakes, which the guns were "laid on" to put them on the "base point." The others were sticks marking small disturbed areas of ground. "What's in there?" I asked.

"We don't know exactly," I was told. "Possibly mines. But we don't like the looks of those spots, and there's been no chance yet to investigate. Healthier just to keep away."

The crew pushed back the camouflage net from the muzzle of the Long Tom. The heavy barrel, which had been depressed out of sight under the net, rose majestically into firing position. Squatting on the edge of the gulch, camouflage still blanketing its flanks, the great gun looked like some oversized mechanical giraffe sitting on its haunches, stretching out its long neck to survey the landscape.

The moon rose from behind a translucent rim of misty hills, and a thin line of silver slid along the gun tube like a sword. A red light drifted up above us; it was a lighted meteorological balloon. By following it with an instrument that measured its speed as it moved, it was possible to apply weather corrections on the flight of shells.

It seemed mysterious and extraordinary to me that a streamlined missile like a shell, making a journey faster than sound, could be blown off its course by the wind. But I had been told that in the projectile's fourteen-mile journey, even the earth's rotation would have time to affect its aim. Already the Abel computer whom I had seen in the Fire Direction Center had allowed for the world to turn fifty yards under the shell's swift path.

The crew helped me plot out camera positions. Each time the gun fired I wanted to get four different effects with four different cameras. It was hard to judge with the eye how far into space the flash from the gun extended, or how much photographic light it gave out. I was particularly eager to get one picture from as far toward the front as practical, to get the fullest possible effect of the muzzle flash. The men helped me choose a position where I would not be blown off my feet by the concussion, and they helped me ease into it gradually, trying it a little farther with each round until we had achieved the desired viewpoint. They gave me cotton for my ears so that I would not be deafened by the blast.

Each time the gun fired, the whole crew turned away from the flash and shut their eyes tight, and at the same time put their fingers in their ears and opened their mouths wide to protect their eardrums from the concussion. Getting the faces of the gun crew in action was an important picture in the series; Padgitt could be trusted to catch this as he had a quick trigger finger. I set his camera with one midget flash bulb to throw a slight illumination on the men's faces. The other two cameras I placed to catch other viewpoints, and the force of relief gunners divided into two groups to man each camera.

The crew chief called out his commands: *Load! Ready!! Fire!!!* The great gun let forth a roar, and each of us from our various locations tried to catch it at the exact instant of firing. Then I ran from my post at the side-forward angle of the gun, watching where I ran in the moonlight so as not to trip over the mine stakes, and changed the films and reset the cameras for the next round. Since there were several minutes between rounds, I had time to figure out new viewpoints, take measurements, and reset the focus between each firing of the gun.

There was so much interest in photography that night that relief crews from Baker and Charlie batteries came up to help during the hours they were off duty. Soon practically everyone not actually engaged in loading and firing a Long Tom was busy holding film packs, moving tripods, handling lens hoods and camera gadgets, helping me get the four cameras set up and synchronized in time for each round from the gun.

In order to catch each picture at the exact second of firing such close timing was needed, and we had so many signals to one another, that finally the boys said: "We think it would be easier if you would give the command to fire."

It isn't very often that a war correspondent gets the chance to command a Long Tom firing at a bridge by Cassino, and I was delighted. So each time the next round was due, I would yell *load—ready—fire* at the top of my lungs, and four pictures would be taken on four cameras while that 155-mm. shell crashed into space.

It was a little after midnight when the Brigadier General of the artillery brigade came along. He had heard that some pictures were being taken, and he dropped by to see what was going on. Everybody was so busy by that time, synchronizing the shooting of cameras with the firing of guns, that no one stopped for formalities with the Brigadier General.

So many camera gadgets were being passed from one man to another that soon the BG found his hands full of film-pack adapters, cable releases, and film slides. By that time the enthusiasm for photography had risen to such a pitch that it wasn't much longer before the General was operating·my camera while I was giving the command to fire.

CHAPTER 17

Invitation to a Big Shoot

THE FIRING mission was completed just before dawn. There had been no counterbattery, and everybody was in a splendid mood. The gang started into the battery CP and told me to come along and have some cocoa. The BG was sitting inside with the computers, all of them holding steaming canteen cups of cocoa.

"I was ready to stop hours ago," he told the others, as I came in, "but I was too proud to quit."

I looked over my exalted assistant with a critical eye and decided that he was my favorite general. He had snow-white hair which stuck up above his ruddy face in sharp little points. He wore an expression as though he had been laughing at little private jokes all his life. Tied around his neck was a voluminous red and white scarf, which I had never seen worn with a uniform before. I asked him about it.

He took it off and showed it to me. It was a red cloth flag, somewhat torn, with a large white circle in the middle—an artillery sign used by the enemy, he explained, in signaling to their own guns whether the aim is short or over. He wore it as a souvenir of what was, to date, his closest call.

He had been with a group of his forward artillerymen during an attack. Affairs had taken a difficult and confused turn, and they were having to do some speedy diving into ditches. In the course of this he found himself cut off from the others and between his own forward artillery and the Germans. Just ahead of him was a group of Heinies, signaling to their own gunners with the red and white flag. The enemy artillery was "bracketing" to perfect their aim, and the General wondered whether he would ever see home again. Suddenly a high-explosive burst from a German gun fell short of its target, and hit right in the midst of the signalmen with the flag. So the General decided, in his words, that "they didn't need it any longer," and with his trophy he made his way back to his own side.

While Padgitt and I tidied up the unbelievably snarled extension wires, tripper cords, and cable releases, put the various lenses back in their individual leather boxes, folded up the cameras, counted and labeled the exposed film packs, and straightened up generally, the BG sat with the crew on the earth bench, batting the breeze as he called it.

They were discussing happily a recent decoration which three of their number had received. Three artillerymen had volunteered to go into a forward area and burn magnesium to make the Germans think we had a gun position there. The men had dug foxholes first, set off the magnesium, and crawled into their holes. The Germans showered the spot with lead, but the men managed to keep alive in their foxholes, and when the barrage quieted down they crept back to safety. Everyone was proud that this unit had thought up the feat and had accomplished it so successfully.

As the talk rambled on, becoming more and more technical, I was impressed with the constructive attitude of these men toward their jobs. Artillery to them was not a fixed science; the posts they filled were not mere jobs. They were always seeking new ways to employ their tools in the service of their country.

I have observed that in branches of the service where the men have this absorption in their work, the morale is correspondingly high. This was particularly noticeable with the tank-destroyer battalion, and with engineers and men in certain other jobs requiring a high degree of skill. With the artillery liaison pilots, who have the attitude of evangelists toward their calling, this creative spirit is outstanding. In these cases there is none of that fatal numbness which afflicts many soldiers.

Possibly the answer lies in being able to see the results of one's work. Even in civilian life, it is a blessed thing to see the purpose for which one works. But in battle, where the stake is life itself, I believe this is a spiritual necessity. It is inevitable that in war there must be thousands of soldiers fitting like chips into a vast mosaic whose pattern they cannot see. And, lacking that inner support which would rise from understanding the deeper purpose for which they serve, they take their hardships severely. But where men have the good fortune to be able to see their niche in the scheme as a whole, they can take a healthier stand

against the ravages of danger. Certainly with these artillerymen, bot
morale and zeal were superb.

By the time the Corporal and I had the equipment neatly packed, an
our caption notes in order, the men were too absorbed in their conver
sation to notice that daylight was streaming through the hole into th
dugout. The Brigadier General was discussing the desirability of syr
chronizing their firing missions more closely with the Air Force. H
wanted to get after the enemy antiaircraft installations which woul
threaten specific bombing missions. The afternoon before, eight B-26'
had been shot down in full sight of the artillery CP. If he knew whe:
the planes were going on a bombing mission in the area reached b
his guns, he could concentrate on enemy flak batteries, timing his a
tack so the Germans would not have the chance to bring up fresh ack
ack guns before the mission was flown. Later that day he was having
group of air officers come up to work over the details.

While this discussion was going on, the firing officer was heating
remarkable object over the coals of a brazier. It was a shell fragmen
the size of a telephone book and almost too heavy to lift. "The night
heard that piece of flak coming my way I called on all the thirty-eigh
Apostles," he said. He had been sleeping soundly with it ever since, h
told me, using it as a foot warmer.

At this point the General turned to me and asked, "How about som
shut-eye?"

I was more than ready. Now that the long, exciting night was over
had suddenly folded up. The boys had arranged for me to have a dug
out to myself, and had equipped it with extra blankets. But the Genera
decided that I should use his trailer, and insisted on swapping with me
I was too sleepy then to take in all the extraordinary features of hi
improvised home, but when I woke up several hours later I realize
what a remarkable trailer it was. The entrance was designed like
refrigerator door in reverse. When you opened the door the ligh
snapped off. No matter how absent-mindedly you might hurry out, i
was impossible to break blackout regulations.

Over the built-in couch was a reading lamp, and in the ceiling wa
a blue night light, as in a Pullman car. The GI five-gallon can, whic
one sees in war areas by the million, had been fitted with a little spigot
You washed in your helmet, according to standard Army practice, bu
a little brace had been devised against that annoying tendency of hel

mets to tip over. Under the helmet rest, moreover, there was a drain.

At the right was a tiny electric coil for heating a small amount of shaving water, and at the left was a larger heater. Little drawback curtains of blackout fabric masked the windows; a built-in desk had compartments for V-mail blanks, air-mail stationery, maps and charts, lighter fluid, and the usual hard candies. The field telephones hung on neat hooks. A ventilator had been built in over the bed, and pictures of an extensive and charming family stood all about on tidy wooden shelves.

I had just finished observing these facilities, and using as many as a woman requires, when the General came to make sure I had everything I needed. "All the comforts of home is an understatement," I commented.

"I don't miss my girls at all," the General told me slyly. "When my aide and orderly get through I can't ever find anything. So I come in and start fishing around for what I want, and it's just like being home."

It was time for noonday mess, and while we ate scrambled powdered eggs in the cellar of Counter-Battery's pink farmhouse the General talked to me about flying OP's. Frequently he made surveys from the air to study the disposition of his guns, and to make sure the boys were on their toes with camouflage. On these flights Captain Marinelli was his pilot.

Recently the Cub pilots had flown a visiting commission of three Russian generals to various points along the front. Lieutenant Mike Strok, who speaks Russian, had acted as interpreter. The BG was impressed at the comprehensive knowledge the Russians had of artillery problems.

During their expedition, the Soviet delegation was taken to see a Prisoner of War camp. It happened that many of the Germans in the enclosure had also fought at Stalingrad. They were dumfounded when they saw the Soviet generals, and they began muttering among themselves. A few minutes later, several of our Hawaiian Japanese soldiers came into the camp, and when the prisoners saw them their demoralization was complete. "We thought you were fighting on our side," they exclaimed.

"Might be a good idea to turn some of those Heinies loose so they could spread the glad tidings back in their own ranks," chuckled the General.

The word had traveled around the artillery post that I was going home soon, and when I finished mess a boy came up and shyly begged me to take four dollars to buy a dozen roses for his girl when I returned.

"Since you're going home so soon," said the General, "I wish you'd call my gal and tell her I'm quite alive and kicking."

"Of course," I said.

"I think a lot of my gal or I wouldn't trouble you to call. Tell her as far as you saw there were no signs of senility or premature decay."

"I'll give her an eyewitness account," I promised.

Then I told the General there was one more thing I wanted to do before I went back to America. I had photographed incoming enemy shells and outgoing "friendly" shells. Before I left I wanted to photograph "friendly" shells landing on enemy territory. Was that possible?

"Yes, that's possible," replied the General. "But it's not always healthy."

However, he consented to arrange it. Within the next few days there was to be a "big shoot." D-Day and H-Hour were of course secret. In fact, they had not yet been precisely set as the date depended on the infantry's reaching certain positions. But it would have to come soon. It was absolutely essential to capture Mt. Trocchio.

Mt. Trocchio was the last razorback peak guarding Highway Six at the end of Cassino valley. As long as the enemy had their OP's on the mountain where they could direct fire on every jeep, tank, and half-track that came through the valley, it was impossible for our infantry to advance into Cassino. A heavy night barrage was planned in the hope that it would win us the mountain.

Already large stores of extra ammunition were making their way to the front. All the guns in the countryside would be trained on that one mountain.

"I've never seen a photograph of that sort taken," said the General. "I don't know whether you'll be able to get anything. But it will really be something to see. I'll send my aide along to help you. Stay alerted so you can leave at a minute's notice. You'll be notified at the proper time."

On our way back to Naples, Padgitt and I stopped at an ordnance depot which our artillery friends had said would be interesting. Here the Monday-evening *Frontepost* was being packed for delivery. I had seen newspapers delivered by foot, bicycle, truck, train, and airplane, but never before by shell.

The Bureau of Psychological Warfare had found 105-mm. smoke shells ideal as news carriers. The smoke candles, used ordinarily for laying camouflage screens for infantry, were removed from the shell casings and replaced with newspapers; just enough of a powder charge was left so that when the shell landed the end would be blown out and the leaflets would scatter. Papers were packed on Saturdays to be delivered on Mondays; deliveries were made according to a rigid twilight schedule. This was to help German soldiers to pick up their papers without being caught at it by their higher officers.

Sometimes outstanding news events called for special midweek bulletins. Extras had been issued to announce major Russian victories, in which case the newssheet pointed out to its German readers on the Cassino front that the Russians were now several hundred kilometers closer to Berlin than they themselves had been.

When our troops were faced by Austrians, a little quiz sheet was shot over the lines with the query: "Who has been sucked dry by the Germans?" And the answer read, "The Austrians—now more than ever." After the next question: "What will happen to Austria after the war?" the bulletin informed its readers that "the United States, the Soviet Union, and Great Britain solemnly declared at the Moscow conference that Austria's independence is to be restored."

Following the third question: "What do Austrians do about it?" it pointed out that already hundreds of Austrians had gone over to the Allies, because "to continue fighting would mean to fight against a free and independent Austria."

Frequently a short lesson in English was catapulted into the German ranks. It was headed *Funf Minuten Englisch* and contained, with parallel translations, such tantalizing phrases for study as:

"Some more coffee, please."

"Where is there hot water?"

"When can I take a bath?"

"I am hungry."

"Thanks for the cigarettes."

On the reverse side of the language lesson was a list entitled:

"*4 Arten nach hause zu kommen*" (4 ways to get home)

"1. See it through and trust to luck." (Under this one it was pointed out that the living are put in again and again, and replacements arrive only for the dead.)

"2. Lucky hit—also called the million-dollar bullet. Rare but altogether efficient. Shouldn't be too high or too low. But often there is only an inch between death and getting home."

"3. Gravely wounded—Cripples get home."

"4. Captivity as prisoner of war." (Here it was stated that prisoners are treated fairly, given good food and adequate medical care, paid in conformity with the Geneva convention, and would be shipped back to Germany after the war.)

This bulletin, and other leaflets like it, was a *Passierschein*, a free pass for Germans who wanted to surrender. When it was persuasive enough, which I was told it frequently was, Germans would slip across the lines waving it over their heads.

One prisoner who had crept through the lines with one of these propaganda sheets turned out to be a portrait painter who had been sent to the front to paint a picture of his CO in action. He did not say whether it was distaste for his commanding officer as an art object, or our psychological warfare, which had made him decide to throw over the whole thing. But he stated quite positively that if there were more single men in the German army, more of them would surrender: the family at home was an ax held constantly over the married men.

However, the major cargo of the propaganda shells was the weekly *Frontepost*—a serious, well-edited newssheet. It contained four pages of straight news, and was as careful to stress Allied losses as successes. This policy seemed to have won the confidence of its readers.

Some prisoners whose homes were in Berlin stated that the only news they got of home came from our paper. It could not have been cheerful news for them; often' it was their only source of information as to the intensity of Allied bombings over their home city. Some recent prisoners had indicated that the *Frontepost* had assumed such a place in the lives of German infantrymen that if we were late with an issue, German soldiers would go along the front lines complaining, "Where is my *Frontepost*? The paper is late today!"

Too big for a courthouse square.

A lanyard pulls about as hard as a sticky door.

Rolling with the punch.

Speaking for 130,000,000 of us.

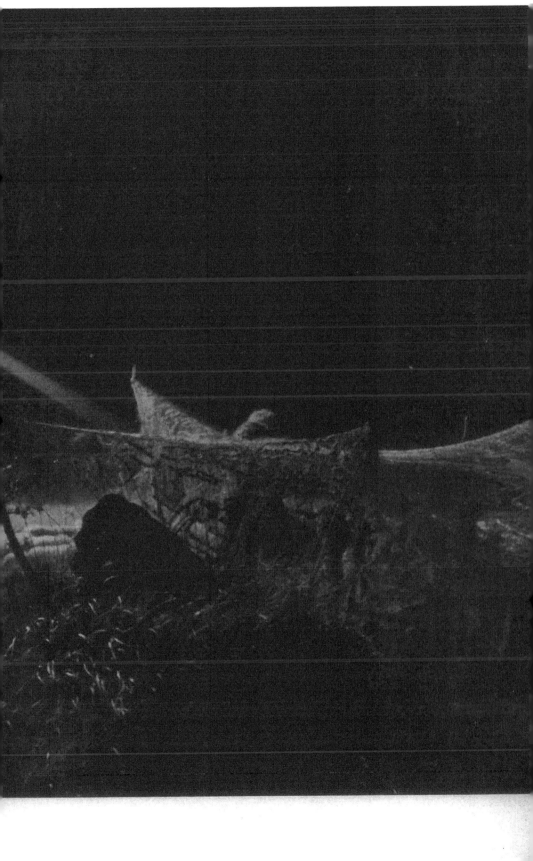

He must calculate how much the earth will turn under a moving shell.

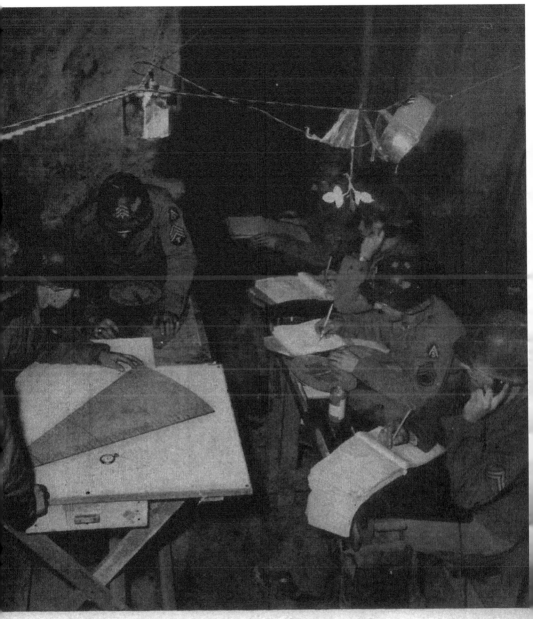

What a city room is to a newspaper, this fire direction center is to a
battery of Long Toms.

The gun flashes in the foreground are from our artillery.

The barrage on the enemy-held mountain in the distance is coming from these
and some 200 other heavy guns.

H-hour was at 5:30 A.M. The barrage lasted exactly one hour.

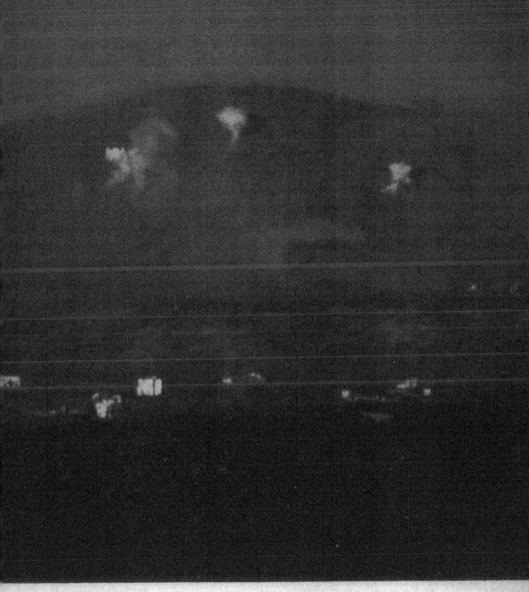

At sunrise smoke shells were fired to provide a smoke screen for the infantry.

The enemy held the other side of the hill and the job of this security patrol was to keep the gun crews from being surprised, while firing or while sleeping.

These were the most forward observers on the Fifth Army front. Their job: to spot enemy movements of men or vehicles and enemy batteries. They relayed the information back by radio phone to the fire direction center.

A thousand yards down the road are the Germans. These observers for mobile guns are watching . . . watching.

Sugar mule, sugar mule, where are you now?

Men, mules, and machines all struggling forward together through mud and enemy fire to capture this lethal curve of the highway. At the end of this horseshoe lay Purple Heart Valley.

CHAPTER 18

Box Seat for a Battle

D-DAY FOR Mount Trocchio was postponed and postponed. I had already obtained my travel orders in quadruplicate, with their BRITISH CONFI-DENTIAL EQUALS U S SECRET designation. Everything except the equipment I would need for the big barrage was packed and ready to go home.

The rains had been steadily pouring down, clogging all operations at the front. The artillery officer at headquarters, with whom I had been told to keep in contact, kept saying, "We feel like a bunch of snails. Come back again tomorrow." And when I came back I would hear more about the weather, and more about the habits of snails. "Snails thrive in moisture," he would tell me. "Maybe we'll get a break and get our firing orders tomorrow. All I know is we'll *have* to make that attack soon, because as long as the Krauts have those OP's, the infantry cannot get into Cassino."

I obtained an extension on my travel orders, and passed the days trying to imitate a snail. Meanwhile the weather brought my faithful Padgitt down with such a severe sore throat that he was confined to his barracks. Then one day at noon the sun came out and I received a cryptic telephone call suggesting that I get my cameras into a jeep within the next twenty minutes and start forward. There was no time to collect Padgitt, and no use upsetting him anyway, since he was probably still too ill to go—though I knew it would be a great disappointment for him to find he had missed out on the big show.

On my way to the front I was joined by the artillery general's aide, Lieutenant Harold Halstead Park, Jr. Lieutenant Park had the tall-dark-and-handsome type of good looks. He was a pleasant young man from Katonah, New York, son of the animal sculptress, Madeleine Park. "H-Hour will be five o'clock in the morning," he told me.

His general had arranged for me to watch the barrage from a forward OP on the top of a mountain that overhung Trocchio and, since we would have a steep climb ahead of us, had also delegated some men to help with equipment. He timed our arrival so as to climb the mountain after dark. The mountainside was under direct enemy observation, and if we had gone up by daylight, the signs of activity on our part would have drawn fire. There was no way the Germans watching through their binoculars could be expected to recognize that I was just a harmless photographer.

The plan was to get me to the top of the mountain first, a climb which would take about an hour. We were to carry only a portion of our equipment with us. Once we were sure that the position gave us the outlook we needed, the men would go back and carry up the rest of the cameras, films, and food supplies.

They would also carry up an artillery "zoot suit" for me—a heavily lined whipcord zipper suit which hung from suspenders like a pair of overalls. This would go on over all my heavy field clothes, which already consisted of two sets of GI long underwear, two sweaters worn under a heavy wool shirt, a field jacket, and a trench coat. My companions were afraid I would have a hard enough job pulling myself up the mountain in all those clothes; the zoot suit could be added later to keep me warm during the long cold hours of the night.

We made our way up the steep crags in the darkness, pulling ourselves sometimes by our hands and knees, and then staggering on without even the aid of the usual red-lensed blackout flashlight. Even this feeble beam, it seemed, might draw fire.

We had to follow a white tape just faintly visible in the dark. The mountain had been so newly captured that our sappers had had a chance only to clear mines out of a slender pathway. The white tape was the characteristic marking indicating mine clearance. We took extraordinary care never to take a step even slightly to the left or right—rather difficult with the amount of crawling and sliding that our rocky climb involved—because we could never tell when a misstep might land us on a mine.

When we reached the top of the mountain, we found ourselves in a grove of ghostlike olive trees clinging to the rocky slopes. It took a good deal of searching to locate our OP, but at last we found it, a perfect little cave with excellent observation toward Mt. Trocchio and across the valley to Cassino.

In the dugout we found a surprising object—a delicate little, antique, gilded Italian chair. I don't know who could have brought it there, or when. It was an astonishing thing, especially since there were only completely wrecked villages for miles around.

Now that I was established in the observation point the boys prepared to go back down the mountain to get the equipment and the food, and Lieutenant Park said to me, "You know, I suppose I ought to leave one of these fellows with you. You wouldn't want to stay here all alone."

I knew there was a great deal to carry, and it was a hard climb, so I didn't feel right about having someone stay behind just for escort duty. I said so.

"Are you sure?" asked the general's aide.

"Oh, no, I don't mind staying alone," I assured him, and he started with my crew down the mountain.

I sat in the dugout and listened. I had been told that there would be only light firing until time for the barrage, as we were only going to be shooting counterbattery. If the Germans shot at us, and thereby revealed a gun position, we would of course chunk back at them. But otherwise our crews would hold their fire until H-Hour.

Perhaps to an artilleryman this was a light night, and maybe our crews were only firing counterbattery, but as I sat there in the coal-black dugout it sounded like a lot of shooting. So I decided to go out and watch. I took the little antique furniture piece, climbed out of the cave, set it on the edge of the cliff, and sat down on my gilded chair to watch the shooting.

Right beneath my feet, at the foot of the cliff, was a row of howitzers sending out sporadic darts of flame. Since I was so high up and so far forward, most of our heavies were in back of me, and I could look over the hills from which we had come and see the muzzle flashes of friendly guns, looking as if people were lighting cigarettes all over the landscape.

The whole valley was clanging with our fire. I could hear our shells, coming from a distance of six to possibly fifteen miles, rushing like locomotives past me toward the enemy. Some of them seemed to be passing actually below the level of my mountaintop, sounding like subway trains rumbling beneath my feet. The rocky slopes picked up the echoes until the mountainsides seemed to be filled with slamming doors. Occasionally I would hear the whoosh of an incoming shell, but the Germans

were aiming less toward the mountaintop than at our troop concentra
tions below.

As I sat there in my gilded chair I began remembering all the stories
I had heard of enemy infantry attempting to infiltrate, and German
patrols slipping through the lines at night. I remembered how they sometimes tried to overpower gun crews or capture forward observers. If
they happen my way, I thought, they're going to be pretty surprised to
find they've captured a woman.

Once I thought I heard voices, but the sounds died away. Another
hour passed. This time I was sure I heard voices. They were coming
closer. I wondered briefly what I would do if I heard them talking German. But soon they were near enough so that I knew they were speaking
English. My crew had brought back not only our food and equipment,
but a tiny oil stove to heat our supper. The general's aide had even carried a portable radio up the mountain so we could listen to the news
broadcasts.

It was very cozy in our little cave. We blacked out the door and the
observation holes with blankets while we heated our supper. We turned
on our radio, and for a long time could get nothing but swing music.
When this was interspersed with German we knew we were listening to a
Nazi propaganda broadcast. The Germans, knowing our boys are
hungry for popular American music, make recordings of our favorite
swing orchestras and feed them back to the Fifth Army front. They play
a great deal of cowboy music, and they specialize particularly in the
latest song hits. The first time many of our boys heard *Pistol-Packin'*
Mama it was beamed from Berlin.

Then a woman's voice, speaking perfect Manhattanese, broke into the
program. "That's Sally," said Lieutenant Park.

"Hello, Suckers," said Sally. "How would you like to be in good old
Wisconsin tonight? It would be nice to be going out to a dance with your
best girl, wouldn't it? But don't worry about your sweethearts. They're
having a good time. There are plenty of men who stayed back in America who can take your girls to dances tonight." And then the German
radio gave us a little Harry James.

Finally we managed to tune in on a BBC news broadcast. We could
hear the clipped British accents of the announcer giving us news of
various war fronts—Russia, the Pacific, and finally our own battle front

—and we heard him say: "Fighting is severe in the Cassino Corridor. The Germans are strongly counterattacking."

"I hope that was last night," Lieutenant Park remarked.

The night crawled on with sporadic firing from both sides. We slipped out to watch it at frequent intervals. At 2:30 we heard the faint hum of a plane overhead. "Piper Cub," said Lieutenant Park. "That's Captain Marinelli dropping propaganda leaflets over the lines."

Clouds were drifting over the stars, and I grew increasingly worried. The moon was due to rise in half an hour, and I was counting heavily on that moonlight for my photographs. But it was much more than photography at stake; I knew our infantry were counting on that moonlight, too.

At half-past four the clouds began breaking and the flattened disk of a three-quarter moon sailed out into clear sky. The pale light gleamed on the white rocky slopes of our mountain and, for the first time, I could distinguish clearly the gnarled shapes of the ancient olive trees which clung so tenaciously to the slope. Their trunks were scarred and battered from frequent shell hits. Many trees were split in two, and the wreckage of broken branches was strewn on the ground.

I set up four cameras on tripods, focused them at infinity (pointing at the moon to do this, for the moon furnishes a convenient check for infinity), and then directed them toward the valley. The general's aide had helped me plot out the camera range on charts, back in the dugout. We had to figure out our bearings carefully to make sure that we were including the proper field on each camera. I wanted everything set in advance so I could catch the very first shell burst of the barrage.

Next we took olive branches and set up a low camouflage screen in front of the tripods. I didn't want anybody mistaking them for machine guns. By that time it was five o'clock, and we kept our eyes glued to our watches and waited.

Everything had become so quiet that it seemed impossible that a whole army had crept into position in the valley below us, awaiting the signal to go. Both the enemy batteries and our counterbattery had quieted down. At 5:29 the earth was deathly still.

And on the second of 5:30, the whole world seemed to open up with a roar. We could hear our shells swooping by like railroad trains. We watched Mt. Trocchio suddenly transformed into a Christmas tree lighted up with candles. Shells were crashing on it in a hail of falling stars.

These star showers fell in gusts like a thunderstorm sweeping along in waves of rain. We would see a cluster scattering over the western base, then a cluster crashing among the central slopes, then a handful sparkling against the northeast crags, and then a dazzling splatter toward the mountaintop.

There was nothing casual about the spacing of these star bursts. Watching the entire barrage, we could observe that each area in turn was being thoroughly blanketed with shells. Each acre of the mountainside had been parceled out among the batteries. Each gun was aiming at the specific area allocated to it.

Some of the shells winked on and off like fireflies as they hit, and some flowered into expanding red smoke plumes. I had heard men in artillery circles refer to covering a certain zone by "firing a serenade," and here it was: this unearthly serenade strumming against the mountain.

As we watched there was a progression of climbing stars spaced, we knew, so as to give our infantry a chance to advance. There could be nothing hit-or-miss about a sequence like this because the barrage had been planned to co-ordinate with the infantry. The battle plan had been laid by the infantry, and the artillery was supporting them in their specific plan of attack.

Toward the end of the hour the shells began crowding closer to the top. Finally there was a constellation of air bursts timed to fling their whirling fragments on the enemy troops below. They shone briefly like red planets hanging over the mountaintop, and then the barrage stopped as suddenly as it had begun.

We glanced at our watches. It was precisely 6:30.

"We've got several of our men in there with the infantry," said Lieutenant Park. "Some of our artillery officers go along with walkie-talkies so if the infantry ask for more fire in some specific spot we can give it to them."

Such a message must have been sent, because after a few minutes there was a new burst of shells on the extreme eastern tip of the mountain, where there must have been a nest of Germans still to be "neutralized."

Again things were quiet, and the valley was lighted only by the moonlight gleaming along shelves of mist.

"The Old Man's down in there somewhere, too," said the general's aide. "You couldn't keep him away from a big show like this."

At dawn we watched something new. Our guns began firing a barrage of smoke shells directed in an even row along the mountaintop. They were throwing a smoke screen to mask our infantry as it stormed forward. It gave a most extraordinary effect. For a time the smoke shells were spaced so regularly along the curved summit of the ridge that Mt. Trocchio took on the appearance of an old-fashioned feather fan, with its row of ostrich plumes curling from the top.

Lieutenant Park heated some coffee. We sat on our clifftop, drinking it from canteen cups and watching the valley grow lighter. The whole battle area was spread below us like a map. As the sun rose, the light touched with blood red the wrecked houses of San Vittore and Cassino. We could pick out the hairpin turns of the road leading from Cassino to the Benedictine monastery just above, and rising over all was the snowcapped peak of Mt. Cairo, looking for a few minutes like a freshly chilled raspberry ice.

A little later the sky suddenly became spotted with dirty black puffs. "Whose ack-ack?" I asked.

"That's Jerry ack-ack," said Lieutenant Park. We could see fighter planes on two levels, but none of them were hit. And below, a little Cub was circling about tirelessly on its lonely mission.

Then the sky was quiet until mid-morning, when we heard a drone overhead and saw what looked like a long, thin line of geese flying toward the mountain. These were our fighter bombers coming to lend their support to the battle for Mt. Trocchio. Suddenly the first one peeled off, and then the next and the next. As they dropped their bombs, the mountaintop began gushing forth gray mottled columns like a smoking volcano.

Then smoke spread over the valley until the whole scene became so obscured that it was impossible for me to take pictures any longer. We worked our way down the mountain, passed a line of pack mules picking their way along a gorge, reached our jeep, and drove back to the artillery Command Post.

At the CP the staff were hanging on the telephones, getting reports from forward. "They shot their last screaming shoot at us last night," the executive officer told me. "Some 170's came whistling overhead just before we started our barrage."

The artillery staff was in a jubilant mood because the attack had gone precisely according to the time schedule. I was told that during the hour-long barrage we had watched, they had shot five thousand rounds. All but a portion of the farthest slope of Mt. Trocchio had been captured. The men were calling it a mop-up action.

The staff officers began receiving reports from reconnaissance planes that German traffic was heavy in the region of San Angelo. Evidently there was a strong enemy movement toward the rear. Two dams had been blown up by the enemy as they pulled out, and the land between Trocchio and Cassino was flooding.

One serious setback had taken some of the joy out of victory. During the first five minutes of the attack, two direct shell hits had been scored by the Germans which wiped out both of our battalion aid stations. Fifteen medical officers were killed, and almost the entire medical staff was either killed or severely wounded. This cost us more than the lives of the medical personnel. Many soldiers died who would have lived if there had been somebody to take care of them during the attack. Purple Heart Valley had taken even more than its customary toll.

We went to mess in the pink plaster cellar, and during lunch the executive officer was called to the phone. When he came back he announced, "I just talked to WigWag, and they confirmed that all of Mt. Trocchio is ours."

During mess, Corporal Padgitt arrived. He had checked with my billet and, finding that I had left, had dragged himself out of bed and hurried forward, hoping to be in time for the barrage. He took it stoically that he was just in time to pack up my cameras.

As I said my good-bys to the general's aide and the rest of the staff, the phones were ringing again. "It's the Old Man," relayed one of the officers. "He says we're going to have an artillery CP up there in no time at all."

Then the officer turned to me. "He's asking if you've been heard from," he said. "He wanted to make sure that you hadn't been hurt, and that you got what you wanted."

"Tell him everything went marvelously," I said. "Tell him I'll never forget him for arranging it for me."

When the staff officer hung up he turned to me. "The Old Man says you must come back to us again. He says to tell you that we regard you as one of us now."

Padgitt and I had a long drive back to Naples, and on the way the Corporal, who was always getting hungry, placed a couple of C-ration cans on the motor under the hood. When we had driven far enough so they were hot we stopped at the side of the road for chow. The Corporal had the whole procedure worked out to a science. With each C-ration can of stew comes a second can of hard crackers. By emptying his cracker can and mine and filling them with gasoline, the two cans set side by side would support a canteen cup of water without tipping and the gasoline when lighted would burn just long enough to boil water for coffee. A small can containing the powdered coffee came packed with the ration.

"When I land in New York," said the Corporal, "I'm going to the Automat with a pocketful of nickels and play it like a jukebox."

"I'll drop in a few nickels for you," I promised.

"How does it feel to be going back to the U. S. A.?"

"Oh, I don't know. When you're a correspondent you get a sort of disease. Always afraid you might miss something."

"Well, I've seen you miss some things you were lucky to miss. When I think back to the jams we were in together and came out of without a scratch! That's one reason I liked to stay near you when Jerry was laying them in. I think you were born part horseshoe."

It is funny how you *do* feel safe with some people and unsafe with others. I had felt very secure with certain people, and unsafe with others who showed that they were frightened. And I had always had a feeling of great confidence with the Corporal. He had never given an inkling that an incoming shell was any more to him than just an incident in a busy day.

For dessert the Corporal brought out an apple and a *cochi* from the fruit supply we kept cached in the back of the jeep. Apples were Padgitt's favorite delicacy and he would bargain for them loudly and strenuously whenever we passed through a town in the rear areas where we could find a fruit stand. His business deals with fruit venders were the only times I ever heard him noisy. But nobody seemed to like *cochis* but me. They looked like overgrown persimmons and tasted like a cross between honeydew melon and peaches. The riper and messier they were the more I enjoyed them.

"After you leave, they'll send me back to guard that same old door in Africa again," said Padgitt.

He reached for a second apple, and selected another *cochi* for me, so soft it barely held together.

"It's going to feel damn cheap to be sitting way back there where it's warm and dry, and where you have a warm bed every night and are fairly sure you're going to wake up in the morning.

"I'll be thinking of the time I put in up here, trying to sleep through that incoming and outgoing mail, not knowing when one of those letters postmarked 'Berlin' was addressed to me. And I'll be remembering those kids we saw up here who—well, I'll feel like I'm not doing a thing to help these guys up here," he concluded.

I wiped the *cochi* off my face and hands. The Corporal continued, "It sure will feel funny to be back out of range."

This was the longest I ever heard Padgitt talk during the five months we worked together.

As we drove back to Naples I said, "Would you like me to look up those Army correspondence courses for you when I get back? The Army must have a law course."

"Gosh, that would be keen," said the Corporal. "I'd sure like to have something on hand to study."

When we arrived in Naples and started unloading the gear, Padgitt asked, "Peggy, when you go home, would you call my mom?"

"Why, I'd love to," I said.

Then I had to refuse a ten-dollar bill he tried to push into my hand. "Listen," I said. "When somebody does something for you every day for five months, the least you can do in return is make a long-distance call."

I was mystified when, without another word, the Corporal dashed off down a little side street. I sat rather impatiently in the jeep, wondering what on earth he had gone to do in such an unexpected manner. Finally he returned with a large package wrapped in coarse paper and string. "A going-away present for you, Peggy," he announced.

I opened it and a coral-pink counterpane of enormous proportions, elaborately machine-stitched in light blue thread, overflowed the jeep. "Thank you," I said. "I'll take it home to my house in Connecticut and shall always keep it."

"I sure thank you plenty for telephoning my mom," said Corporal Padgitt.

CHAPTER 19

One More Purple Heart

THE CORPORAL was not slated to stay in front of that door in Africa for very long. Before I flew back to America I found out that the quiet efficiency he had displayed while working with me had attracted some notice, and that a new post was being planned for him.

I had been back in New York only a few days when I received a V-mail letter in the neat printed hand which Padgitt always used: "Everybody seems to be very happy about my future and think I am very lucky, but they are all so Mysteriously secretive about it."

This was shortly followed by another V-mail, which read: "Here I am again over in Italy. I didn't think I would ever come back to it again but my Uncle changed my mind."

From another source, however, I learned that it was not Uncle Sam who changed his mind, but the Corporal himself. The attractive new post had been offered to him (it had to do with photography, I believe, and incidentally it was "out of range"), but simultaneously, his infantry company had been ordered to the front and the Corporal had decided he should not leave his outfit now that they were moving up.

The next letter came from Anzio. "It's as noisy as New Year's Eve," Padgitt wrote, "and this time I'm not taking pictures. I'm on a different job now. This one really isn't a bit more dangerous than what you and I were doing."

By which I knew it was.

"So long, and don't lose that rabbit's foot," the letter ended.

And don't lose yours! was my silent hope.

A little later I learned from Major Papurt, also at Anzio, who had hunted for four hours through foxholes to find Padgitt, that the boy was living in a little glade 250 yards from the German lines. "He is in an I & R (Intelligence and Reconnaissance) Platoon," wrote Pappy. "He likes his job."

These communications crossed letters of mine referring to the Army courses of study and the five pounds of law books (following Army postal regulations) which I had weighed and measured for the Corporal. When Padgitt received all this data he replied, quite logically, that on the beachhead they had plenty of other studies, and right now he would not be able to carry the books. As he put it, "Here at Anzio you carry nothing but your gun, plenty of ammunition, and a lot of hope."

The next letter was brief. "I'll do my best to tell you a few of my experiences from here but not in this letter. I will write you two days from today (I hope)."

It was only when I glanced at the top of the V-mail form that I happened to notice that it came from Jess Padgitt, Sergeant.

There was no letter in two days. When there was no letter in two weeks I was really worried. A glen 250 yards from the enemy is not exactly a health resort, even if you do like the work.

Then a letter arrived from one of his buddies. "Sergeant Padgitt asked me to write to you and explain why he isn't able to write. He was wounded in action and is in the hospital. He has the best of doctors. Some of us go to see him every day and take him anything he asks for. There isn't much I can tell you, but I assure you he is going to be as good as new."

It was a fortnight later that I received a note in laboriously printed letters, which came evidently from the left hand of Sergeant Padgitt himself. He had four doctors, he wrote, and they had operated on him four times. He thought they were about finished with him now. "They say I almost kicked the bucket, but I fooled them."

The mortar fragments he had picked up hadn't caused him too much trouble. It was the machine gun bullet which passed through his upper chest into his shoulder, severing the nerves of his arm on the way, that had done most of the damage. The healing process would take time; but the nerves would regenerate.

"My right arm is paralyzed," the awkwardly penciled characters explained, "but it shouldn't leave me crippled. One collarbone and a few ribs broken, two large muscles cut, two other places where shells tried to get through, but I can still eat."

I later learned more details, again from Pappy who, with his unfailing kindness, had looked up the boy in the general hospital. It was from one of his buddies, wounded at the same time but less seriously, that Pappy got the full story.

Sergeant Padgitt had shown considerable leadership in the action. He had been in command of one unit of a combat team whose mission was to clear the Germans out of a house. Their orders were not to shoot until they were positive they had been seen, and all went well as they made their way undetected past two machine-gun nests. However, within fifty feet of the house they were observed by the gun crew of a third machine-gun nest, and this crew immediately threw up a flare. There it hung over Sergeant Padgitt and his men, making everything as bright as day.

By the light of the flare they could see that machine-gun nest only ten feet in front of them, and in the next instant hand grenades were bursting around them, "knocking them half silly." Sergeant Padgitt gave the order to fire, and he and his six men poured that Kraut gun position full of lead from their tommy guns. Its crew gave them no further trouble.

But this was only the beginning. Mortar shells started breaking in on them as they continued to advance. Two shells falling close wounded two of the men. A third shell, still closer, blew Padgitt's tommy gun to pieces in his hands. He paid little attention to the fact that he had lost not only his gun, but also the use of his right arm.

The Sergeant continued to lead his men forward. The fact that their position now was known made the situation pretty desperate for them, but it served to aid the other two sections of the team which were approaching the German-held house. While Padgitt's unit was drawing fire on itself, the other two units flanked their objective. Then the order to return was given.

To get back, the squad had to run the gantlet of the two machine-gun nests past which they had slipped on the way out. But by now their position had been so thoroughly advertised that return was little more than a prayer and a hope. During the hellish journey, two of their men were captured, and Padgitt picked up more mortar fragments, this time in his back. Yet despite his severe wounds the Sergeant brought himself and most of his squad back.

When they finally made it to their own lines, the wounded were rushed to the hospital. This was none too soon in the case of the Sergeant, who was told later by his doctors that in only a few more minutes he would have drowned in the blood which was filling his lungs. "But here I am," Padgitt sized it up, "with one arm up in the air.*

Padgitt's loyal buddies felt that in fulfilling the mission in the face of such opposition their Sergeant had covered himself with glory, but the Sergeant said all he got covered with was "blood and mud."

"They tried to cover me with six feet of dirt and a white cross," he told the Major, "but I hadn't kissed my mom and my girl friend good-by so I just refused."

"I always knew he had what it took," Pappy wrote to me.

* Just as this book goes to press an additional note comes in on Sergeant Padgitt: he can now move his right arm four inches and his unit has received a citation.

CPSIA information can be obtained
at www.ICGtesting.com
Printed in the USA
BVHW091114030322
630479BV00006B/572

9 781258 507336